Church, City, and Labyrinth in Brontë, Dickens, Hardy, and Butor

American University Studies

Series III
Comparative Literature
Vol. 50

PETER LANG
New York • San Francisco • Bern • Baltimore
Frankfurt am Main • Berlin • Wien • Paris

Marilyn Thomas Faulkenburg

Church, City, and Labyrinth in Brontë, Dickens, Hardy, and Butor

PETER LANG
New York • San Francisco • Bern • Baltimore
Frankfurt am Main • Berlin • Wien • Paris

Library of Congress Cataloging-in-Publication Data

Faulkenburg, Marilyn Thomas.
  Church, city, and labyrinth in Brontë, Dickens, Hardy, and Butor/ by Marilyn Thomas Faulkenburg.
    p. cm. — (American university studies. Series III, Comparative literature ; Vol. 50)
  Includes bibliographical references and index.
  1. English fiction—19th century—History and criticism. 2. City and town life in literature. 3. Literature, Comparative—English and French. 4. Literature, Comparative—French and English. 5. Brontë, Charlotte, 1816-1855—Criticism and interpretation. 6. Dickens, Charles, 1812-1870—Criticism and interpretation. 7. Hardy, Thomas, 1840-1928—Criticism and interpretation. 8. Butor, Michel. Emploi du temps. 9. Labyrinths in literature. 10. Church in literature. I. Title. II. Series.
PR868.C53F38   1993   823'.809—dc20   92-27279
ISBN 0-8204-2058-1   CIP
ISSN 0724-1445

Die Deutsche Bibliothek-CIP-Einheitsaufnahme

Faulkenburg, Marilyn Thomas:
Church, city, and labyrinth in Brontë, Dickens, Hardy, and Butor / Marilyn Thomas Faulkenburg.—New York; Berlin; Bern; Frankfurt/M.; Paris; Wien: Lang, 1993
  (American university studies : Ser. 3, Comparative literature ; Vol. 50)
  ISBN 0-8204-2058-1
NE: American university studies/03

The paper in this book meets the guidelines for permanence and durability of the Committee on Production Guidelines for Book Longevity of the Council on Library Resources.

© Peter Lang Publishing, Inc., New York 1993

All rights reserved.
Reprint or reproduction, even partially, in all forms such as microfilm, xerography, microfiche, microcard, offset strictly prohibited.

Printed in the United States of America.

Acknowledgements

I had an idea when I began this study. That idea soon yielded to another, and that to yet another and another until the original idea was forgotten. For a number of months, as my research took me off in many directions at once, I found myself lost in a labyrinth of texts that sometimes did and sometimes only seemed to contradict each other. It was Kent Bales, Professor of English at the University of Minnesota, who helped me find a common thread in all the reading. He guided me along the way better than any Ariadne.

Other professors at the University of Minnesota played a role. Charles Sugnet, for example, always checked my tendency to draw the facile or untested conclusion. It was he who introduced me to the writing of Michel Butor. Professor Gordon Hirsch is especially responsible for insights into the novels of Dickens and Brontë. He was generous in offering advice regarding questions of style. Professor Yi Fu Tuan offered insights that helped to shape the introduction. The Sisters of St. Agnes, in whose community I was a member for many years, granted me time away from the duties of teaching to pursue an academic career. Among them I credit Sister Muriel Tarr, now deceased, for instilling in me a love of scholarship.

I owe special thanks to my brother Len Thomas and his wife Nancy. Back in 1977 before PC's were available, they used a VYDEC text editor to prepare this manuscript for binding as a doctoral dissertation. That was in the days before spell checkers and laser printers.

Once again today I have Nancy Thomas to thank for text preparation. I am also grateful to my husband Al who believes in me as a writer.

It was Ronald Jansch, O.F.M. Capuchin who suggested that I submit this manuscript to Peter Lang Publishing. Seventeen years had passed since he had read the manuscript and he still remembered and valued it. Naturally, I am grateful to him. Mrs. William Hewlett, whose husband co-founded Hewlett-Packard, has been my patroness in this project. Without her financial support, this book would still be a manuscript. I met her at Menlo College, where I teach and where she is a board member.

I have named only those who had a direct bearing on the content and physical appearance of this book. If I started to name all who had an indirect influence on my thinking and writing, I'd need another book. I hope they already know of my gratitude.

Contents

1. Church and City Relationship
   —Church and City in History and in Fiction 1
   —Mythic and Symbolic Foundation 14

2. *Villette*—An Irresolvable Tention 35

3. *Edwin Drood*—A Boneyard Awaiting Resurrection 63

4. *Jude the Obscure*—An Unattainable Dream 87

5. *Passing Time (L'Emploi Du Temps)*—A Life-Sustaining Myth ... 109

Afterword 136

Bibliography of Works Cited 139

Bibliography of Works Consulted 144

1. Church and City Relationship

—Church and City in History and in Fiction—

In reading novels of the nineteenth century, one is impressed by how images of the city and church define world views. The nineteenth century witnessed city and church transformation unparalleled before or since in the history of Western Europe. In his book *Contrasts*, A.W. Pugin called his Victorian contemporaries' attention to the startling difference between the typical medieval town and its nineteenth century development. Through illustrations he shows how the typical town has been transformed from a shapely, steeple-dominated prospect in the Middle Ages to a nineteenth century progeny, an amorphous, smokestack-cluttered landscape.

In Great Britain, three-fourths of the population lived in large cities at the end of Queen Victoria's reign as opposed to one-fifth of the population at the turn of the nineteenth century. In fact, the word "urbanize" was not used before the late nineteenth century. To put the matter concisely, "in the rapidity and extent of the urbanization of her growing population, Great Britain was without peer."[1] Concomitant with the growth of cities was the simultaneous impact on the place and authority of the church. Formerly at the center of city life culturally, if not topographically as well, the church now faced the challenge of expanding with the city or stagnating at its displaced center. By the time of the Industrial Revolution, cities no longer crystallized around their central religious edifices as they had in the Middle Ages. Then the church was the center of city life, not only topographically, but morally as well. It was the church that made and enforced the laws by which city life was ordered. By the nineteenth century, however, a heritage of Renaissance humanism, seventeenth century empiricism, and eighteenth century rationalism exploded in an industrialism that changed the face and manner of city life. Accordingly, J. Hillis Miller can write:

> Though it is impossible to tell whether man has excluded God by building the great cities, or whether the cities have been built because God has disappeared, in any case the two go together. Life in the city is the way in which many men have experienced most directly what it means to-live without God in the world.[2]

Although the concepts of city and church have been considered extensively in literature from many different viewpoints, such studies have often examined city and church as entities independent of each other.[3] In fact, however, the definition of one often includes or presupposes the existence of the other. In legal terms, for instance, the definition of the city, at least into the seventeenth century, required that it be an episcopal see.[4] In the eyes of a religious mystic, to consider another definition of the city, "the true Christian commonweal or city is the Church and no temporal body."[5] Viewed from an historical perspective, ancient cities were often planned to reproduce by imitation an observed cosmic order. For early man, "reality was achieved through the imitation of a celestial archetype, by giving material expression to that parallelism between macrocosm and microcosmos without which there could be no prosperity in the world of men."[6] Geometrically, the square or circle was the preferred shape. The center, or *axis mundi*, was considered a sacred space, forming the point of intersection for imaginary lines extending in the four directions of the compass. From this "holy of holies," the rest of the city received its orientation. It was considered holy because here communication was established between heaven and earth as well as between earth and the underworld of the dead. Here, too, divine power entered and diffused itself throughout the kingdom. According to Allcroft, the circle was considered a magic area because it guaranteed sacred protection from the devil who was believed to lurk in the corners.[7]

With the coming of the Industrial Revolution and its concomitant scientific technology and genius, however, many cities grew in response to economic and practical demands rather than religious and ideational ones. The transformation of the city from an imitation of a celestial archetype into urban sprawl is both anticipated and bemoaned by nineteenth century men of letters.

In general, the effect of this displacement of the central church and the city around it by unintelligible and random agglomerations of the city surrounding it is the subject of this dissertation. Although the poet and literary critic were adversely critical of the coming age of cities too large to be comprehended or controlled, the novelist merits special recognition as "the" social voice reflecting and directing the consciousness of the masses.

In defining the genre of the novel, J. Hillis Miller goes so far as to define it as the "art form called into being to deal with the conditions of urbanized life."[8]

The prospectus which follows looks first at some novels in which the city as theme is predominant, then takes an overview of work considering the church primarily; and finally gives brief consideration to some novels that illustrate correspondence of city and church and the gradual breakdown of that order.

The failure of the city to meet the needs of its citizens is often attributed to its lack of cohesiveness. John Ruskin, visionary, critic, and literary genius, whose life and writings span the nineteenth century, expresses the ideal relation of church and city as follows: "In all healthy states, the city is the central expression of the national religions, the throne of its legal authority and the exponent and treasure-house of its artistic skill." According to Ruskin's way of thinking, however, the Biblical vision of the city as holy, as a "going up of the tribes to the mountain of the Lord: in the psalmist's words, is in reality a "going up of the tribes as by instinctive drainage into a slime-pit of central corruption."[9]

Writers of the time who were visionaries as well as social reformers in spirit chose the city as central metaphor to express the effects of such a physical "slime-pit" on the citizen's psychology. They agree that the picture is one of moral disintegration. With Ruskin they voice a theme common to their century's literature when he describes cities as "mere crowded masses of stone, and warehouse, and counter," which are "to the rest of the world what the larder and cellar are to a private house."¹⁰ The city which once served as the focal point of social and religious significance has become a storehouse of the merely pragmatic rather than the aesthetically meaningful. Consequently, Ruskin bemoaned the impossibility of finding "true architecture" in the modern city, that is, architecture which is a visible manifestation of the soul of its builder and which expresses delight in God's work rather than man's.

Literary artists often looked to the former city in such utopian schemes as those of Virgil, Plato, and Augustine as a measure against which to judge its architectural realization in the modern age. Even before the turn of the century, William Blake is dreaming in poetic revery of building a Jerusalem in England's green land even if only a fragment of England's garden remains out of which to build such a city. In his dreaming, Blake envisions England as a garden, a defined area in which the presence of the sacred might yet be symbolically enclosed and acknowledged.

Wordsworth, too, sees beauty in the city, but in a city that communicates with field and sky. When the river is allowed its own will and the city is clothed in nature's sunlight, then London is a "City," a vision of heaven on earth. When the city's heart is quiet, when its heart beats a rhythm with nature's universal law, then the city merits praise. But when its "mighty heart" sets up a rhythm contrary to that of nature, it becomes a heart that misdirects its citizens in a labyrinth of congested streets and soot-choked air as described in "Lines Composed Upon Westminster Bridge." Consequently, cities in their ordinary state, "the fallen state of Albion," are "fallen images of the Emanation Jerusalem."¹¹

City life, a theme central to the novel which gained in popularity as cities increased in number and size, receives symbolic shape as a means of defining social and psychological values. At the turn of the nineteenth century already, Jane Austen presented the dichotomy between what the city pretends to be in contrast to what it is in actuality. For her characters, the city from outside appears as a promised land of culture. Once inside its walls, however, one's integrity is threatened by an enveloping complexity and dishonesty bound up with the business called living. In *Northanger Abbey*, for instance, Bath is the scene of duplicity and betrayal. Likewise, *Mansfield Park*, in the novel of that title, is a shelter from the corrupting influence of the city. While leaving the country for the distant city is symbolic of the fall, returning to the country again signifies redemption. A parsonage in the country is always the ideal for Ms. Austen.

If in the novels of Jane Austen direct experience of the city reveals the illusive nature of the fruit so appealing from afar, William Dean Howells writing at the end of the century and from a new country presents an interesting contrast. Both a profuse writer of novels himself as well as critic who set the pace and standards for realism in the American novel of his time and after, Howells may be considered as a representative voice of morals and manners in the late nineteenth century novel in America. Instead of running from the city or letting oneself be overwhelmed by the city's diversity of manners, a Howells protagonist will exercise a kind of Faustian defiance in mastering its labyrinthine turnings, and will make the city his home.

In *A Hazard of New Fortunes*, for example, Mrs. March, admitting that she loses a sense of individuality in the city, finally convinces herself that anonymity in the big city is a good thing. To remain unknown in the city is to preserve one's privacy as well. A labyrinth, after all, need not always be threatening; for its tortuous windings offer privacy and darkness, values to be retained as long as they are balanced by social communion and the light promised in the completion of one's journey to its center and safe exit again. For the March couple, accident and exigency, attendant consequences of the city's growth, are seen as healthy challenges of city living. Sordid as New York may be, Howells does not fail to see the city as an invitation to growth in moral uprightness. In A *Modern Instance*, to cite another of his novels, Boston has a corrupting influence on the Hubbards (the young couple from a small town hoping to achieve fame in the city), but one that might have been averted had the Hubbards found its religious center as Ben's mother has; for while she is numbered among Boston's socially elite, she remains morally upright and unpretentious.

A contemporary of Howells, but more like Jane Austen in his concern for the city's adverse effects on the psychology of his characters, Henry James presents an unfavorable picture of Boston and New York. Unlike Howells, who equates city expansion with cultural progress, James presents the city as a maze of institutionalized causes to be won and traditions to be preserved at the expense of personal fulfillment. In *The Bostonians*, for example, society uses Verena's cultural identity and religious devotion to attain its own political and social ends. Olive Chancellor, the embodiment of the feminist movement, for example, wants nothing less than to sacrifice Verena as a martyr to the cause of feminism. Recognizing the one-sidedly masculine quality of the city, Olive assumes the burden of making the city by shaping one of its more promising citizens into her idea of a feminist paragon. On the other hand, there are those who endeavor to capitalize on Verena's crowd-drawing charisma to augment their social prestige. Although she used her religious gift sincerely, others merely capitalize on its pragmatic, cause-furthering value. The city, once regarded as a symbolic expression of man's desire for communion between heaven and earth, is not portrayed as wholly earthbound. James includes the scenery of a Cape Marmion as a nostalgic reminder of a pastoral retreat almost vanished, but Verena's choice is limited to that between Boston and New York. Had she chosen Boston, Verena would have been possessed by Olive's form of institutionalized femininity. Instead, she lets herself be whisked off to New York City, a place embedded in "immemorial accumulations of stagnant mud,"[12] an image that echoes Ruskin's impression of fallen Venice and Dickens' description of London in the opening pages of *Bleak House*. In either case the picture is more demonic than heavenly.

If one is tempted to search James's novels for a more promising vision of the city in Europe, that search will not prove fruitful. European cities differ merely in outward appearance. Underneath the trappings of sophistication and culture, Rome, Paris, London, and Florence threaten one's personal integrity. In *The Portrait of a Lady*, the climactic awakening of Isabel Archer takes place in a city of ruins where buildings in their continuing state of collapse only convince Isabel the more of the insignificance of her sorrow in comparison with a city whose history of human suffering is so long and vast. Burial sites suggest only death rather than potential resurrection as they did in their foundations, churches having been founded on grave sites as affirmations of life through death. Acquaintance with Rome is dear to Isabel for its record of suffering and ruin rather than triumph. In *The American*, Urbain, the pretentious, narrow-minded snob, personifies the city, as his name suggests. In fact, Newman, upon meeting him, "felt a sort of impulse to step backward as you do to get a view of a great facade."[13] The city for James represents a state of mind, a container of attitudes and sentiments grown stagnant with age. *The Wings of the Dove*, another novel that pits America against Europe, depicts the European city as a stone colossus, a labyrinth which imprisons and deadens rather than frees or gives life. For Milly, London is a lion's den and Venice a prison fortress.

It is significant that the city grew out of the burial ground as an act of faith in life's unending nature; for expansion that loses touch with these roots, as has been the case since the nineteenth century, is expansion cut off from death and burial as potential symbols of life. Fragmentation of traditional values and alienation from one's urban neighbors are the results of denial or disregard of one's need for communion with one's past as the source and center of meaning and orientation in the present. A sense of feeling at home in the church of the living which extended its life into the surrounding cemetery has given way to fear as death becomes increasingly a private affair divorced from city life. No longer is the cemetery a place for business transactions, dancing, gambling, socializing, and commerce as it was in the Middle Ages.[14] Consequently, in a novel like *The Rise of Silas Lapham*, the protagonist, feeling more isolated from life in Boston than on his farm, beats a retreat back to the country. In one of Howells' later novels, however, the possibility of retreat itself is gone; for when in *A Hazard of New Fortunes* Dryfoos permits the digging of oil wells on his property, his farm and family plot, his most precious possessions, are permanently destroyed. Subsequently, Dryfoos is a displaced person in a city expanding haphazardly without concern for individual needs.

Not only does the city divorce itself from its dead; even the farm's burial plot has been obliterated. Having a grave on one's farm is a curious phenomenon in America, a practice which was "unknown in Europe before the mid-eighteenth century and with few exceptions was rapidly abandoned."[15] The fact that Howells can refer to such a practice so nonchalantly indicates a difference in cultural values between tradition-conscious Europe and nature-worshipping America. In the Romantic era of America's history, the dead were often envisioned as asleep in the bosom of Mother Nature from whom they came and into whose bosom they returned. This kind of veneration of the dead differs markedly, however, from that of European tradition in which the departed were considered as intemporal members of the temporal city. In Europe the dead were traditionally walled within the city until city expansion forced them out. In America, that tradition was never strongly adopted. Whereas the dead in America of the nineteenth century are portrayed by Howells as venerated and remembered only by their immediate families, the dead in medieval Europe, before widespread city expansion and sanitation laws changed the situation, were absorbed by the city and most particularly by its church where they formed an "intemporal image" of the temporal city; "for the dead have gone through the moment of change, and their monuments are the visible sign of the permanence of their city."[16] When oil wells obliterate burial sites in America and industry crowds out cemeteries in Europe, one can see that veneration for the dead as part of nature or as an extension of the city is at a low ebb.[17]

As the hazard to public health became known and the need for space grew with urban expansion during the nineteenth century, the dead were gradually moved to the outskirts of the city. It should also be noted that romantic nature worship so popular in America had something to do with the move. This change was accompanied by an increased experience of alienation among the living themselves. In the nineteenth century alienation becomes an increasingly prevalent topic of concern. Dostoevsky captures the essence of this psychological state in the Underground Man. In the midst of a metropolis, he is nameless, faceless, and superfluous. In *Notes from the Underground*, as in *The*

Double, Dostoevsky portrays St. Petersburg as a city in which one face can address another face only in the act of writing, which is essentially a solitary act. As in most of his novels, Dostoevsky embraces St. Petersburg as his setting, where he "moved with purposeful familiarity amid a labyrinth of tenements, garrets, railway yards, and tentacular suburbs."[18] In American fiction this theme is forcefully portrayed in Poe's "Man of the Crowd" and Hawthorne's "Wakefield." Mirroring the city they inhabit, many of Dostoevsky's characters are psychological and emotional cripples divorced from the healthy life that has its roots in the soil. It is a "misfortune to live in Petersburg" declares the Underground Man, "the most abstract and premeditated city on earth."[19]

As the city continues to mushroom without its necessary nourishment from communion with its sacred dead, city spokesmen perceive it as a parasite feeding on itself. In its twentieth century manifestation as a sterile, death-dealing ash heap, the city is lamented by city-dwelling poets such as W.H. Auden, e.e. Cummings, and T.S. Eliot. Novelists who echo the theme include D.H. Lawrence, F. Scott Fitzgerald, Theodore Dreiser, and James Joyce. Of the major nineteenth- and twentieth-century writers who have embodied the city as a labyrinthine confusion in their fiction, I have cited only a few, but enough to illustrate the point that the phenomenon of burgeoning cities devoid of cosmological orientation and significance in the nineteenth century landscape is given ample expression in belle lettres.

In conjunction with the disorganized sprawl of cities, the nineteenth century witnessed a shift in the outward appearance and function of churches. Not surprisingly, one can find a great deal of fiction that expresses a concern with religion and its place in a rapidly changing society. Voicing the religious philosophy of the century in poetry, Arthur Clough's "The Latest Decalogue" expresses succinctly the growing dichotomy between one faith professed and another lived. Tennyson's poetry shows compassion for those who suffer from a sincere religious skepticism, and Francis Thompson's "Hound of Heaven" celebrates a faith that grows out of rebellion against traditional modes of worship. Matthew Arnold transferred his allegiance from a church-regulated faith to a culture-preserving art. His dream was to restore the "sweetness and light" of a spontaneous Hellenic classicism lost by the law-conscious tradition of Hebraic Christianity. Like the city in its failure to provide adequate authority and direction, so too, the church of the time proved inadequate as a means of preserving and transmitting religious truth. Bereft of living symbols to draw it to a common creed, society consciously rejected one vacuum only to enter unwittingly into another.

The Gothic novel, a genre originating in the eighteenth century, but which grew in popularity and influence throughout the nineteenth, exploited Roman Catholic ritual and practice to create an atmosphere conducive to terror, horror, and suspense. Reacting against a medieval frame of mind that enforced conformity through fear- and awe-inspiring practices, Gothic novelists undermined the credibility of saints' legends and depicted the church's God as "a contrivance, demonic and irrational."[20] Medieval, ecclesiastical settings portrayed to the protestant mind the powers of darkness and damnation rather than the hope of life and redemption. Although it is true that some of these Gothic writers were concerned with instructing and imparting morals, as well as with exciting the emotions, the church atmosphere invoked was intended not to inspire faith in church attendance or doctrine, but rather to probe the irrational and demonic side of human psychology.

Although the Gothic novel offered an escape from the everyday world of consciousness and used church accouterments for this purpose, writers of romance and realism looked more to the world of daydreaming and wakeful consciousness in their consideration of the church and its place in the city. Among early American romancers, Hawthorne was concerned with original sin and man's need to redeem both civic and ecclesiastical institutions. In *The Marble Faun*, for instance, a city girl from Boston describes St. Peter's Basilica in Rome as the material home of religion. However, St. Peter's evokes from her a judgment in favor of Puritan simplicity rather than the Roman Church's pomp and splendor which is all body without soul. Hilda remains true to her New England form of Puritanism in all its characteristic emphasis on interior conversion and starkness of ritual, even though she performs the ritual necessary to receive the sacrament of reconciliation in this center of Roman Catholicism. What is important to her is the spirit of religion rather than its external form. As will be seen later, *Villette* records a similar scene. It is the institutional church's communal value that these heroines seek but find to be inadequate.

A novel closely related in motif to Hawthorne's romance is Harold Frederic's *The Damnation of Theron Ware*, which also pits one church against another. The protagonist, a Methodist minister, disgusted by the ignorance of his parishioners and humiliated by the petty politics of his church, seeks the cultural advantages and rich heritage of the neighboring Roman Catholic Church. The church in the country village seems to Theron both psychologically and spiritually destitute, and as a consequence he gravitates to the city-oriented sophistication of the Catholic Church. Introduced to its scriptural scholarship and lured on to New York City by its lady Celia, a devoted daughter of the Church, Theron's enlightenment consists in an awareness of his damnation in a city where the center does not hold, where demonic meaninglessness in the periphery is countered by deception at the center. If Theron experiences frustration in the throes of Methodism's trivial pragmatism, he discovers an equally damning deception at the core of Catholicism's cultural heritage.

Man's need for a center that will give purposeful direction to his own life within the larger context of a community of shared belief is a theme satirized by Howells in *The Leatherwood God*. Into Leatherwood's camp meeting (itself a temporary center removed from the community's topographical one) walks a man who convinces the community that he is God incarnate. Subsequently, in a series of events that parody the life of Christ, this man becomes the wish-fulfillment of the local community. Suggested is the possibility that churches are shells demanded by man's weakness, and consequently appeal to some ultimate authority that will give his life purpose and direction, even if that authority is arbitrary. The man who will dare penetrate into the heart of religion's structure and worship is rare, for his fear of finding the core empty may be well-founded. Where does one turn when a center-denying society proves itself an illusory guide to self-fulfillment here as well as eternal joy hereafter?

In America, a church largely without either institutional effectiveness or political power has for a model the church in Western Europe with its long tradition of interdependence of city and church in that medieval church leaders were temporal as well as spiritual lords. Consequently, even though the church has generally lost religious credibility by the late nineteenth century, its influence as a political establishment continues to hold. Writing about the church in England, Anthony Trollope explores the institutional church as a political extension of the state. In his novels clergymen contend for power over the appurtenances, the material rewards of "spiritual offices." Similarly, Samuel Butler explores the destructive influence of accumulated conventions within the church and its ministry. In *The Way of All Flesh* retreat from the city as well as the church seems to be the best possible solution for a fallen Pontifex family. One must please himself and disregard the unanswerable. Stendhal, in *The Red and the Black*, modifies the theme, but continues to explore the church as a road to power when poverty and obscurity block a political route. By the end of the century, concerns with church-inspired worship and ritual are replaced by questions of power and economy in the church as well as the city.

In varying degrees novelists as diverse as Emily Brontë, George Eliot, and Flaubert explored the inadequacies of church structures to meet the social and spiritual needs of its members. In *Wuthering Heights* the church lies beyond the worlds of both heath and hearth, standing as it does beyond the limits of both Wuthering Heights and Thrushcross Grange. Here it remains empty in a state of disrepair and without a pastor. Then, too, in *Madame Bovary* the heroine finds convent walls suggestive of the inadequacy of life and the immanent decay of all things. This home of her escapist daydreaming serves as prelude to a life of disillusion. In *Middlemarch* Dorothea remembers Rome as "the city of visible history, where the past of a whole hemisphere seems moving in funeral procession," and recalls St. Peter's Basilica in all its splendor of mosaic and red drapery as a "disease of the retina," a magnificent external display without soul, a reaction reminiscent of Hilda's in *The Marble Faun*. In the former case, however, there exists a dichotomy between Dorothea's judgments and her creator's. For while her heroine's limited vision sees only images of death and disease, Eliot herself is more sympathetic. With her broader vision and greater maturity she perceives the "growing soul" in historic shapes, and traces out "the suppressed transitions which unite all contrasts," and therefore can still pronounce Rome "the spiritual center and interpreter of the world."[21]

A positive voice for the church sounded in the twentieth century is that of D.H. Lawrence in *The Rainbow*. For Will the church is a "sign in the heaven, it is the Spirit hovering like a dove . . . over the earth." The church is "the perfect womb" and "a great involved seed" whose "flower would be radiant life inconceivable." On the other hand, Anna his wife, resenting her inability to share Will's ecstatic response to the symbolic values of church architecture, calls its structure "the ultimate confine." And finally, Will himself must admit that "he tended it for what it tried to represent, rather than for that which it did represent." In all these images the church's centrality is emphasized. Whether enclosed in a womb or seed, the church nevertheless frees rather than stifles in its ideal state; for from its womb all life emanates, blossoms, and returns again as seed to be reborn. Like Jude Fawley's Sue, the "Bridehead" who personifies Christminster in Hardy's novel, Will, in relation to the church, "was like a lover who knows he is betrayed, but who still loves, whose love is only the more intense. The church was false, but he served it the more attentively."[22]

Well-known critical studies have already been published demonstrating the significance of both the city and the church as literary motif in the nineteenth century and early part of the twentieth.[23] This study differs from what has already been done in that it pursues the subject of church and city in their symbolic correspondence. Although the novels of James Joyce would suit this theme nicely, much has already been written on the subject. Other novels, however, which explore the interdependence of church and city in thematic terms, have been neglected and therefore deserve consideration. In general, the four novelists selected for this study demonstrate a gradual fragmenting of religious and social solidarity between church and city. Novelists for whom church and city interrelate topographically as well as symbolically in defining the religious and social tenor of the nineteenth century include Charlotte Brontë, Charles Dickens, and Thomas Hardy. This study will examine their portrayal of the city as a threatening labyrinth with the church as its collapsing center. Although church and city are spatially joined in these novels, the spiritual mortar holding them together is crumbling. Michel Butor, a contemporary French novelist, embodies in his novel *Passing Time* a culminating expression of this theme, which will be explored in the final chapter of this study.

— Mythic and Symbolic Foundation—

Novelists commonly describe the city in labyrinthine terms. The changing definition of the term is significant. To the ancients, the labyrinth connoted paths of intricate deviation leading eventually to the center for the initiated from which demons were excluded by the very device of the labyrinth. In the Middle Ages that center still held in the guise of walled towns with a centrally-located church giving order to the whole complex. In the nineteenth century that center begins to be eclipsed by secular institutions and by the twentieth century, novels question even the validity of presupposing that a center exists to be found. Consequently, in considering the interrelationship of church and city, one is led to consider the labyrinth with its circular core as symbolic foundation of the city. Before considering the correspondence between center and periphery, it will be necessary to consider each concept separately in its symbolic uses and meaning. Correlations between the dynamics of the labyrinth and those of the city will then be more apparent.

According to anthropologists, geographers, and psychoanalysts, the geometric concept of circularity is one of the most universal and basic to men's understanding of the world. Universally it is the symbol of wholeness and harmony. It is, according to Yi-Fu Tuan, "a recurrent motif in the arts of ancient eastern civilizations, in the thinking of ancient Greece, in Christian art, in the alchemical practices of the Middle Ages, and in the healing rites of some non-literate peoples." As an archetypal image of the reconciliation of opposites, the circle also appears in the design of traditional and idealized cities. Concepts of center and periphery are likewise universal, since people everywhere show evidence of structuring space by placing themselves at the center "with concentric zones . . . of decreasing value beyond." Related to circularity, according to Tuan, are the concepts of open and enclosed. Whereas openness often signifies freedom, adventure, light, and society, closure suggests the womb, security, privacy, and darkness. When one or the other becomes threatening, however, the victim experiences either agoraphobia or claustrophobia.[24]

One of the most ancient uses of the circular as symbol remains even today in the visible traces of burial grounds. Because these grounds became temple sites, the cemetery served as the foundation of the city with the temple as religious and legal center of authority. As a consequence of studies conducted particularly in England and the British Isles, A. Hadrian Allcroft has cited evidence which demonstrates that architectural features of burial grounds for dawn man were most frequently circular. As containers of the bones of the venerated dead, these grounds took on a religious character. Another feature of these circular burial grounds was a vertical image located at the center. Whether tree, rock, or pole, this vertical object served symbolically as a link between heaven and earth, between the microcosm of man and the macrocosm of the universe. In short, "religion and burial being inseparable, the same circularity which marked the burial place marked also the *temenos*; tomb and temple had one common plan."[25]

The circular burial ground with vertical dimensions, then, was a place of ritual veneration with cosmic orientation. And as such, it represents the bare bones of an architectural structure which eventually received the name church. The word *church* itself shows in its etymology this connection between circularity and consecration. In Old English, *church* is derived from "cirice" meaning circle. Just as burial grounds were set aside, i.e., consecrated for religious ritual by the presence of bones, so too the church altarstone used for the ritual sacrifice of the death-resurrection mystery must contain the bones of a venerated, deceased member. The idea of a plot of ground taking on a sacred character is developed by Mircea Eliade in *The Sacred and the Profane*. According to this thesis, man encountered the world as differentiated: land from sea, and sky from both, for instance. But ways of imposing meaning by categorizing were invented only as part of an historic process. Until these ways of imposing significance evolved, the earth was amorphous, or to use Eliade's term, profane. What designated certain times and places as sacred in opposition to profane, then, was their being differentiated from the mass, set aside or consecrated, as the word sacred implies. Consequently, meaningful assembly with the presiding presence of ancestors in consecrated burial ground came to be seen as a sacred act. Furthermore, since scientific findings have established the circular burial ground as the first meeting place chosen because of its sacred character, burial ground bears a real relationship to the structure later known as the church. Even after circularity disappeared as a common feature of burial grounds, the dead continued for some time to occupy the area immediately surrounding the church. This practice remains even today in country churches. Similarly, cathedrals entomb their venerated dead beneath the nave. City churches, largely discontinued burial around them due to lack of space and for hygienic reasons. Nevertheless, the notions of church and cemetery remain closely associated culturally even today. For modern churches without crypts still have bones in their altarstones and often in their cornerstones.

Because circularity has always been associated symbolically with perfection and the vertical with transcendence, it is appropriate that these geometric shapes be incorporated into the church with its orientation in the supernatural and absolute.

Circularity is associated symbolically with the ideal city as well as the ideal church, however. And, in fact, the two are often associated together as one large circle: the church as the center; the city organized concentrically around it. According to Lewis Mumford, the city had its birth in the burial ground, just as the church did. "Urban life," he writes, "spans the historic space between the earliest burial ground for dawn man and the final cemetery, the Necropolis, in which one civilization after another has met its end."[26] Like the church, then, the ancient city received its birth and special character from the burial ground that constituted its center.

Examples of circular cities founded on burial sites are still with us in the world of fact as well as fiction. Rome, for example, was supposedly circular at its founding "with the *mundus* (the place of departed souls) at the center."[27] Even today Rome is called the Eternal City because it is the reputed seat of Christ's vicar on earth and capital of Western Christendom. This city derives its greatest significance, then, from its being the center of the universal church. Moreover, St. Peter's Basilica was built on a cemetery; and tradition has it that the basilica was built on the site because St. Peter was buried there, the basilica erected over his tomb.[28] Writers of novels who used to their advantage this convergence of the sacred and secular include Henry James, George Eliot, Marcel Proust, and Nathaniel Hawthorne.

In the Christian era one must also consider Jerusalem, which was placed at the center of the world in medieval maps. The wheel maps of the Middle Ages, with Jerusalem located at the hub of the wheel, "expressed the beliefs and experiences of a theological culture."[29] This city, like Rome, is also envisioned as a church in its designations as "Heavenly Jerusalem," "New Jerusalem," and "City of God." Moreover, medieval man depicted the temple of Jerusalem at the center of a circular, walled city.

Circular models also guided the founding of relatively recent cities in history. Paris, for example, was "concentric in pattern and focused on the Cathedral of Notre Dame on the isle de la Cite."[30] Other medieval cities circular in topographical orientation and in which the cathedral occupies a central location include the following: Toulouse and Limoges in France; Cologne, Hanover, and Frankfort-am-Main in Germany; and the cities of Buda in Hungary and Vienna in Austria. In most instances, the medieval city core included the presence of a cathedral or church. For the word "cite" or city "referred to the initial ecclesiastical nucleus."[31] These churches, in turn, were either founded on burial sites or enclosed relics of the dead after the structures were completed. Although the foundations of London, laid before the Middle Ages, are not circular, St. Paul's first cathedral was built on a Roman burial site.[32]

In the world of philosophical and theological speculation, Plato's utopia as well as St. Augustine's City of God are based on circular plans. The former combines the circle with the square, while the latter is purely radial. Literary cities portrayed as circular, often with church as center, expressed man's desire to translate heaven to earth. For example, in Marcel Proust's *Remembrance of Things Past,* the town of his childhood is remembered as resembling a medieval town "as scrupulously circular as that of a little town in a primitive painting."[33] Patterned on the image of perfection, the city ideally was to transcend the vagaries of life and reflect the predictability of the cosmos.

Often, too, these cities were surrounded by circular walls, which, before they were used for defenses, were designed to suggest completeness. While signifying wholeness, walls also served to fix the limits of the city. Within these walls, man's life acquired a sense of direction and purpose. According to Yi Fu Tuan, "the wall was the clearest expression of what the city builders took to be the limits of their domain."[34] Mumford also emphasizes that walls were used as constructions for defense purposes only late in their history. He also cites the importance of church bells in determining the city's limits. Beyond their sound, one was also beyond the city's boundaries and in that area designated as profane.

Contrary to later attitudes that idealized the country, early conceptions idealized the city. According to a German proverb of the Middle Ages, "'City air sets a man free.'" To philosophers of Aristotle's time and after, the city stood for a perfect society. Heathens lived in the country or on the heath; peasants (*pagus*) or pagans lived in the rural districts.[35]

Combining the horizontal and the vertical, the circular city aspired toward an order based on the vault of heaven itself, and in its aspiration came to symbolize that order. In the same way, the church was also viewed as image of the cosmic order. In Byzantine church architecture, for example, the vault of the church was an image of heaven with the floor as paradisal earth. The dome as vault of heaven was preserved through Renaissance and into modern times. Public gestures of man's desire for the transcendent, expressed by the church in ziggurat, pyramid, steeple or temple, has its counterpart first in the church as the center, then in its monument and fountain at lesser "centers." With their vertical/horizontal tension united in the circle construct, city and church symbolize the "antithesis between transcendence and immanence, between the ideal of disembodied consciousness (a skyward spirituality) and the idea of earthbound identification."[36] A sense of vertical striving is tempered by a horizontal call to rest.

Both church and city, then, acquired their rudimentary beginnings within the circular burial ground as place of religious ritual and communal assembly. The labyrinth stands in conjunction with circularity as well in its combination of the vertical and horizontal, signifying perfection. Although not all labyrinths of fact or fiction are circular in shape, the ritual dance associated with them always includes circular movement, indicating their basically circular nature. The general construction of the labyrinth consists of a central area circular in form surrounded by a series of concentric, winding paths intended to confuse the uninitiated.

According to the myth of Theseus,[37] which expresses the mythico-religious significance of the labyrinth, the center was a sacred space. Within it, the Minotaur (half-man, half-bull) signified the union of mortality and immortality (the bull being a symbol of divinity for the ancients). In slaying it, Theseus performed an act of defiance even while fulfilling a requirement of a religious cult. According to this cult, it was necessary that the bull, surrogate for the king-god, be slain in the king's stead, thus insuring the king's continued life as well as the lives of his subjects. Like the ambiguous nature of the Minotaur (god-man) as well as the labrys (double-bladed axe) with which the Minotaur was slain, the myth has a double interpretation. According to one theory, Theseus performed a saving act by slaying the Minotaur because in doing so he guaranteed the people's lives.[38] In another interpretation, however, Theseus was a usurper in that he embodied the Greeks' hatred of the Cretin bull-cult.[39] By slaying the Minotaur he symbolically destroyed that cult, displacing it and substituting in its place that of Athena and the cult of the ram.

Whatever the correct interpretation, it is clear that the labyrinth itself was a center of religious ritual; it was circular in structural orientation; and it celebrated the death/resurrection mystery in a fertility cult. In all these elements it resembles in nature and function a role later played by church and city. Like the church as locus of the celebration of life and death mysteries, the labyrinth was the locus of man's attempt to "overcome death and renew life." According to C.N. Deedes, it was in the labyrinth that "the living king-god went to renew and strengthen his own vitality by association with the immortal lives of his dead ancestors."[40] Communion with the dead was also the purpose behind burial rites celebrated on burial sites. Evidence in the remains of stone circles in England and the Scandinavian countries demonstrates the relationship between circular burial ground and labyrinth. "When we come to examine some of the stone circles of Scandinavia," writes Deedes, "we find that they are actual labyrinths, conforming in design to the plan of those on the coins of Knossos."[41]

While there is evidence to establish a connection between burial ground and labyrinth in their common significance as consecrated ground, there is also a similarity between labyrinth and city. If that relationship can be demonstrated, all the links of the chain will have been joined relating city to church, labyrinth to both, and circularity as characteristic of all with its roots in the burial ground. The question, however, still remains: What is the relationship between city and labyrinth?

The labyrinth, related as it is to church through its association with burial ground, has a more direct relationship to church as well as city in its medieval representation in cathedrals themselves. As W.H. Matthews has pointed out, medieval churches contain labyrinths in art on floors and walls. Although some are called "ways," others have the name "Jerusalem" inscribed at their centers. A labyrinth has also been found with the words "Sancta Eclesia" at the center. Conjecture is that these labyrinths served as miniature pilgrimages to holy cities for those who could not make the actual trip. A "Chemin de Jerusalem" could be walked with one's index finger on the wall if one could not traverse the roads on foot.[42] Not only the church, but the city as well began as a magnet drawing people together to celebrate mystery; the city, too, was "the goal of pilgrimage."[43]

Various pseudonyms for labyrinths also establish a connection between them and cities; "Ruins of Jerusalem," "City of Nineveh," "Walls of Jericho," and "Babylon" are some of the names given to labyrinths.[44] Frequently these labyrinths were given some form of the name Troy. This latter name is of interest particularly in its association with the stone circles of Scandinavia and the earthworks of Britain. It has been reasonably concluded that the bull-cult reached Troy by means of trade routes between the island of Crete and the mainland of Asia Minor. Moreover, a legendary source attributes the fall of Troy to the labyrinthine dance of Ariadne performed around the walls of the city while the Greeks wheeled their wooden horse through the gates.[45]

Not only are labyrinth and city joined by historical evidence; the two are related conceptually as well. A tension between exclusion and inclusion characterizes both labyrinth and city. While the center is a place enclosed, it threatens to become claustrophobic for one enclosed there. On the other hand, while its winding passageways promise the possibility of extension, the labyrinth's external windings protect the center from violation by the uninitiated in the same way that the burial place was protected from grave robbers by intricate passages. According to Paul Kuntz, "the labyrinth was able to protect a city, a tomb or a sanctuary, but in every case, it protected a magical-religious area which excluded those not invited or initiated."[46] The center was a place secluded, while the periphery protected it from invasion.

Besides the tension between exclusion and inclusion, labyrinth and city embody a similar tension between injunction and permission. While injunctions take shape as laws designed to protect the community and regularize worship, permissions contain the more vital designation of possibilities and freedom. Exposure and seclusion, permission and injunction, then, are some of the psychological dynamics of the architectural construct of both city and labyrinth, each with its sacred core surrounded by peripheral deviations.

For the city this core often took the shape of a citadel with its law court and temple; for the labyrinth, it was the bull-ring of ritual celebration. Just as cities often had circular walls enclosing them, the labyrinth had "a circular crenelated enclosure."[47] Related to both city and labyrinth, the injunctive nature of laws as reflected in visible walls, served to define the interior space of city and labyrinth as sacred or set apart. Citadel and center asserted symbolically man's desire to overcome death, to unite heaven and earth, to join the transcendent and the immanent. In their life-giving powers labyrinth and city were a common "means of bringing heaven to earth."[48]

Having their common source in ground consecrated or set aside for the celebration of the mysteries of life and death, city, church, and labyrinth have all undergone a cyclic development: "Ashes to ashes . . . ." As the labyrinth remains today only as a suggestion of some unrecoverable past in its uncovered architectural ruins, so too the city of old has met its death as a means of organizing life. Ashpits of industrial waste and uncontrolled expansion characterize the necropolis of the nineteenth century and after. Likewise, medieval piles are no longer accessible to modern man as his bible in stone. By the time of the Industrial Revolution, material profit had pretty well supplanted ritual celebration and dialog as the purpose for the city's existence. Charlotte Brontë, Charles Dickens, and Thomas Hardy are the three novelists selected for this study because their novels reflect this changed and changing state of affairs in interrelationship of church and city from early to late nineteenth century. Although these three novelists are not the only ones whose works reflect this changing relationship, they are representative.

A twentieth century writer who masterfully weaves the symbolism of city, church, and labyrinth into Hebraic and Hellenic world views is Michel Butor. Influenced by the writings of John Ruskin, Marcel Proust, and James Joyce, Butor illustrates in his verbal tapestry the entropic state to which the correspondence of city and church has been reduced. As buildings, they are dead. As patterns which temporarily help the protagonist's search, they do have some efficaciousness. In consciousness, they are still alive. As a way of integrating his personality into the city's, Butor has his central character, Revel, struggle to make the city his own by adoption. Revel fails, however, to mediate between map and diary, city and self. Concerned during the daytime with the business of translating his mother tongue into a foreign one, Revel spends his evenings hopelessly trying to correlate the city he maps by bus with its supposed replica on paper. The more frustration builds, however, the more Revel becomes immersed and entangled in Bleston's demonic excrescences. Intrigued even as he is alienated, Revel keeps his diary. In the words of Raillard, "C'est contra cette usure et cette exlusion douloureuse que Revel batit son discours."[49] To demonstrate the end toward which the novels of Brontë, Dickens, and Hardy tend, I discuss Michel Butor's *Passing Time* first in this introduction, even though the lengthier consideration of his novel forms a later chapter of this study.

The Old Cathedral, once located at the heart of the city, has been replaced by a New Cathedral, which resembles a museum more than a church. Yet even the New Cathedral is being overshadowed by a commercial center under construction. Together, city and church comprise a city of Cain rather than a New Jerusalem.

The city as setting for Revel's frustrated and confused wandering is "un espace architectural defini par le labyrinthe et le cercle, formes figurees de l'egarement et de le repetition,"[50] that reflect a societal view of the industrial city in addition to one man's state of mind in relation to it. Influenced by a Hellenic as well as a Hebraic tradition, Revel sees Bleston as a mythic labyrinth with himself as Theseus. As Revel sets out to unravel the city's tangled maze, he perceives himself as an avatar of Theseus who will thread on paper the labyrinth Theseus traversed on foot. Given a city, however, whose labyrinthine accretions are accidental rather than planned, Revel is engaged upon a mission whose difficulty dwarfs that of his mythic mentor.

During the course of the previous century, writers such as Charlotte Brontë, Charles Dickens, and Thomas Hardy also envisioned the city in labyrinthine terms. From *Villette* to *Edwin Drood* to *Jude the Obscure*, one can perceive a gradual regression of a possible correspondence of city and church, from relative order to chaos, from a celestial vision to an infernal realization, from a center found to a center only mentally conceived.

Charlotte Brontë's *Villette*, for example, is organized in terms of an architectural interdependence between church and city, a correspondence culturally presupposed. At the outset the protagonist believes there is indeed an external order within which she will be able to find a home and self-identity. When Lucy walks along London's streets, for instance, her initial sense of labyrinthine wandering is dissipated by her privileged view of the city from the heights of St. Paul's dome. London as "a Babylon and a wilderness" yields to her modified impression of security and protection when the city is viewed from a distant perspective. What may initially look like a hostile city of blind alleys and darkness without light, becomes through insight an architectural pattern bounded by a river and green land.[51]

Villette, too, provides shelter at its core (significantly a church building) after Lucy Snow's initial experience of the city as a threatening labyrinth in which she is pursued by strange men and where she is lost without a guide. Here, as in London, a church structure gives to the city a sense of objective orientation and provides respite from the hostile, dark streets outside. The church is the city's prominent landmark by which Lucy orients herself. Unfortunately, however, Lucy is soon to discover the illusory nature of what she temporarily perceives as authoritative comfort.

As in *Villette*, church and city in *The Mystery of Edwin Drood* receive their identity from their structural interrelatedness. Cloisterham, for example, is a city that takes its name from its cathedral. Likewise, the cathedral receives what life it still has from the city. Unlike the center of the labyrinth, the ritualistic place of the dying and rising god, Cloisterham is a boneyard not only at its center, but in its city extension as well. The pattern of living provided for the city's breathing inhabitants is one out of the dead past which denies change and therefore life. Jasper is the protagonist who suffers most because of his inability to repress, to live as though patterns supposedly effectual in the past are adequate for the present.

For both Brontë and Dickens the city is a fearful place because, while it provides a cultural pattern by which to order one's life, that pattern demands too great a self-surrender. Fearing exposure, both Lucy Snowe of *Villette* and Jasper of *Edwin Drood* deny or repress their personal, psychological needs. Although the modern city is generally thought of as the place for self-expression because one is free from censorious neighbors, it is not the case in Villette or Cloisterham. Anonymity, so common now, was less easy to achieve in the earlier church-oriented and smaller cities where one was known by membership and association.

Thomas Hardy's *Jude the Obscure* shares similarities with both *Villette* and *Edwin Drood*. Like Cloisterham, Christminster is a city which is defined by its church structure, and, like Villette, its periphery is characterized by labyrinthine byways. Both Cloisterham and Christminster are cities of the dead which contain only the relics of some former culture irretrievably buried with the bones of its former founders and men of history. Like Lucy Snowe in *Villette*, Jude Fawley fears moral contamination by the city's sorcery. Arabella Donn, daughter of a pig farmer, is the Circe who threatens to compromise Jude's longing for the pure "bridehead" of Sue, who symbolizes the holy city itself. Unable to live without the vision of a holy city believed to be attainable in Christminster, Jude condemns himself to frustrated wandering around excluding walls that supposedly contain a center of cultural wealth and the promise of personal fulfillment. Ironically, as a stone mason Jude helps restore the very walls that exclude him simply because he refuses to relinquish his dream of an existing center of cultural and religious wealth that needs safeguarding, even if he himself is excluded from sharing in it. Eventually, when forced by economic necessity to defer that dream further, Jude turns to selling confectionery churches as a baker supplying a consumption-oriented city market. While Jude sustains his dream with mortar and bread, however, the city itself continues to reject him.

Like a mythic center of the labyrinth, the church (which is the historic center of the city in Western culture) is a fearful place in its realization not as a life-giving force, but as a death-dealing reality. Self-surrender, confession, and purification, the motifs explored in *Villette*, *Edwin Drood*, and *Jude* respectively, are all dying experiences more than life-giving ones for the protagonists concerned. That the cycle can be completed, however, and life renewed by retracing the thread through the labyrinth, is a tenet of the novels of Brontë and Dickens, if not of Hardy in his *fin de siecle* novel, at which time despair inevitably prevailed when man discovered that the universe was indifferent to his psychological plight.

All three novels are taken to be roughly representative of the gradual breakdown between the correspondence of church and city during the nineteenth century. Writing during the first half of the century, Brontë presents the metropolis as a labyrinthine network. In *Villette*, the protagonist is torn between her preconceived notions regarding the city and her actual experience of it. Although church and convent continue to occupy central positions architecturally and topographically, thus conforming to her vision of a Bunyanesque City of God, church buildings are no longer central as the city's moral or cultural guardians. For her, church structures are only temporary stays against the labyrinthine confusion beyond their walls. Neither church nor city provides Lucy with functional symbols of authority. Where one is too restrictive, the other is too prodigal.

If clear lines of authority and a sense of divine sponsorship between church and city are breaking down in *Villette*, their disintegration and demise are more marked in *Edwin Drood* and *Jude*. Although the name of the church extends to include the city in both *Edwin Drood* (Cloisterham) and *Jude* (Christminster), cohesion holds only in name. Geographically and architecturally churches become an anachronism, a mere reminder of their medieval foundations in a world where "the word 'church' did not mean solely the church buildings, but the entire space around the church."[52] Geographically and architecturally churches remain dominant structures in the landscape, but culturally and morally economy and social prestige rule. For Dickens the true church is a spirit residing within the person, so that Tartar's private rooftop garden metaphorically issues a call to moral transcendence more effectual than that of the institutional Cathedral tower. By the end of the century the process of disintegration reaches its nadir in Hardy's *Jude*.

For all practical purposes the prophesied "City of God," the promised "New Jerusalem" is an historic museum for the antiquarian or the culturally elite. Christminster serves neither Christ nor people. The city's taverns are the true centers where the need for social communion and celebration is met. In labyrinthine terms, the city is no longer (if it ever really was) a sacred space whose peripheral windings exclude diabolical forces. Instead it is a maze without central orientation or sacred character. Or, if the center protects, it is a bastion only for those inheritors of privileged positions who exploit them for merely social purposes. During the course of the nineteenth century, visionary concepts of the city as a labyrinth for the initiated, with the church as sacred center surrounded by peripheral city walls excluding demonic forces, died. In the present age the city is still conceived of as labyrinthine, but as a labyrinth without plan or sacred center, a labyrinth without meaning. Inverting the twelfth-century definition of God, Bleston is a personification of the demonic its archetypal labyrinth was built to exclude. If God is "a sphere of which the center is everywhere and the circumference is nowhere,"[53] Bleston is a labyrinth whose center is nowhere (because multiplying continuously) and whose circumference is everywhere (because expanding indefinitely).

Man, the builder of cities to transform the profane, becomes man the demon who is trapped by his own creation. The mythic labyrinth was created to protect the initiated and confuse demons who dared entry. In the modern labyrinth of the city, however, the building of the city itself is demonic, since no one is among the initiated; for one neither knows its plan, nor knows if there is one to know. Any order perceived in the city is a creation of man's own imagination.

In *Passing Time* Revel mentally adopts Theseus and Cain as his guides through Bleston. As threader of the labyrinth and founder of a city respectively, these two heroes are eminently qualified to assist him. Although reference to such mythic heroes enables Revel to draw parallels between his situation in the modern labyrinthine city and theirs in the ancient one, these parallels are no more than a temporary stay against a paralysis of the will and amnesia which he fears will submerge him in Bleston's entropy. To find and seize the thread is symbolically "to return to the source across the confusion of fatal forgetfulness of the path one has trod."[54] Although such a thread provides Revel with the temporary assurance that life is a stable, predictable order, each correlation made between his situation and that of his mythic guide Theseus is undercut by succeeding events that invalidate even the possibility of repetition as a way of escape out of darkness and into light. In its realization in the modern city, "the labyrinth is an empty one, without center, in which the investigator has to do only with his own chalk marks."[55]

Once the labyrinth was significant of man's participation in divinity, should he pass successfully through its tortuous and secret way, a passage which constituted initiation. Now, however, it is "a symbol of man's insecurity and of his efforts to find a center of meaning to his existence, but he is lost within the infinite number of passages that consciousness brings to his awareness.[56]

Notes

1. Eric Lampard, "The Urbanizing World," in *Victorian Cities*, Dyos and Wolff, eds. p.4
2. J. Hillis Miller, *The Disappearance of God: Five Nineteenth Century Writers* (Cambridge: Harvard University Press, 1970), p.5
3. Studies in which the church is the predominant theme include the following:
Henry Adams, *Monte-Sainte-Michel and Chartres* (Garden City, New York: Doubleday and Co., 1959
Sister S. Agnes Heeney, "The Cathedral in Four Major New England Authors: A Study in Symbolic Inspiration," Dissertation, University of Pennsylvania, 1957
K.S. Inglis, *Churches and the Working Classes in Victorian England* (London: Routledge and Kegan Paul, 1963)
Standish Meacham, "The Church in the Victorian City," *Victorian Studies*, XII (1968)
John Ruskin, *The Stones of Venice, Introduction*. Charles Eliot Norton (New York: Charles E. Merrill, 1891) 2 vols.
John Ruskin, *The Bible of Amiens* (New York: John W. Lovell, 1877)
Ernest Panofsky, *Gothic Architecture and Scholasticism* (New York: Meridian, 1951)
Augustus Welby Pugin, *On the Present State of Ecclesiastical Architecture in England* (1843). Reprinted, London: Butler and Tanner, 1969)
Augustus Welby Pugin, *The True Principles of Pointed or Christian Architecture* (London: Henry G. Bohn, 1853)
Vincent Scully, *The Earth, the Temple, and the Gods: Greek Sacred Architecture* (New Haven: Yale University Press, 1962)

Studies dealing predominately with the city as theme include the following:
John Betjeman, *Victorian and Edwardian London:* (London: B.T. Batsford, 1969

Fustel de Coulanges, *The Ancient City: A Study on the Religion, Laws, and Institutions of Greece and Rome*, Trans. Willard Small (Boston: Lee and Shepard, 1874)

R.E. Dickinson, *The West European City* (London: Routledge and Kegan Paul, 1961)

H.J. Dyos and Michael Wolff, ed. *The Victorian City*, 2 vols. (London: Routledge and Kegan Paul, 1973)

E.A. Gutkind, *Urban Development in Western Europe: France and Belgium* (New York: Free Press, 1970)

Kevin Lynch, *The Image of the City* (Cambridge: M.I.T. Press, 1964)

Lewis Mumford, *The City in History: Its Origins, Its Transformations, and its Prospects* (New York: Harcourt, Brace and World, 1961)

Richard Sennett, *The Uses of Disorder: Personal Identity and City Life* (New York: Knopf, 1970)

Christopher Tunnard, *The City of Man* (New York: Scribner's, 1953)

Max Weber, *The City*, trans. Don Martindale and Gertrud Neuwirth (Glencoe: The Free Press, 1958)

David Weimer, ed. *City and Country in America* (New York: Appleton-Century-Crofts, 1962)

Frank Lloyd Wright, *The Living City* (London: Oxford University Press, 1958)

Charles Williams, *The Image of the City* (London: Oxford University Press, 1958)

    4. H.J. Dyos and Michael Wolff, *The Victorian City*, (London: Routledge and Kegan Paul, 1973), xxvii.

    5. Charles Williams, *The Image of the City* (London: Oxford University Press, 1958), p.111

    6. Paul Wheatley, *City As Symbol* (London: H.K. Lewis and Co., 1967), p.10

    7. A. Hadrian Allcroft, *The Circle and the Cross* (London: Macmillan and Co, 1930) II, p.380-381.

    8. J. Hillis Miller, *The Disappearance of God*, p.4

    9. E.T. Cook and Alexander Wedderburn, ed., *The Works of John Ruskin* (London: G. Allen, 1903-12), xxx, p.156.

    10. Cook and Wedderburn, xix, p.24

11. Williams, p.62

12. Henry James, *The Bostonians* (New York: Holt, Rinehart, and Winston, 1945), p.157

13. Henry James, *The American* (New York: Holt, Rinehart, and Winston, 1966), p.130

14. Phillippe Aries, *Western Attitudes Toward Death*, trans. Patricia M.Ranum (Baltimore: Johns Hopkins University Press, 1974), p.23

15. Aries, p.96

16. Aries, p.74

17. According to *Anthos: Landscape Architecture Quarterly*, this trend of divorcing the dead from the living is again being reversed in the twentieth century. Tombstone and flower show the "oversaturation indicative of general affluence," which is being gradually replaced, at least in Europe, by cemeteries which preserve the natural landscape and invite the living to commune there for contemplation and quiet recreation. See *Anthos* Nos. 3,4, and 15. Quotation from Erwin Rehmann,
"Cemeteries: A Sculptor's Thoughts," No.4 (1969), pp.1-5

18. George Steiner, *Tolstoy or Dostoevsky*, (New York: Alfred A. Knopf, 1959), p.198

19. Fyodor Dostoevsky, *Notes from the Underground* (New York: New American Library, 1961), p.93

20. Leslie Fiedler, *Love and Death in the American Novel*, rev. ed. (New York: Dell Publishing Co., 1966), p.36

21. George Eliot, *Middlemarch* (Boston: Houghton Mifflin, 1968), pp.143-44

22. D.H. Lawrence, *The Rainbow* (New York: B.W. Heubsch, 1922)

23. Asa Briggs, *Victorian Cities* (New York: Harper and Row, 1965) J. Hillis Miller, *The Disappearance of God: Five Nineteenth Century Writers* (Cambridge: Belknap Press of Harvard University Press, 1963) David Weimer, *The City as Metaphor* (New York: Random House, 1966) Alexander Welsh, *The City of Dickens* (Oxford: Clarendon Press, 1971) Owen Chadwick, *The Victorian Church*, Part I (London: a.c. Black, 1966)

H.V.Routh, *Toward the Twentieth Century: Essays in the Spiritual History of the Nineteenth* (New York: Macmillan, 1937)

Margaret M. Maison, *The Victorian Vision: Studies in the Religious Novel* (New York: Sheed and Ward, 1961)

24. Yi Fu Tuan, *Topophilia: A Study of Environmental Perception, Attitudes, and Values* (Englewood Cliffs: Prentice-Hall, 1974), p.17

25. A. Hadrian Allcroft, *The Circle and the Cross* (London: Macmillan, 1930), I, p.22

26. Lewis Mumford, *The City in History: Its Origins, Its Transformations, and its Prospects* (New York: Harcourt, Brace, and World, 1961), p.7

27. Tuan, p.153

28. *Encyclopedia of World Art*, VIII (London: McGraw-Hill, 1962), pp.324-349; p.527

29. Tuan, p. 41

30. Tuan, p.159. For geometric significance in town planning see John Archer, "Puritan Town Planning in New Haven," *Journal of the Society of Architectural Historians*, 34 (May 1975), pp.140-149

31. Robert Dickinson, *The West European City: A Geographical Interpretation* (London: Routledge and Kegan Paul, 1951), p.252

32. T.G. Bonney, *Cathedrals, Abbeys, and Churches of England and Wales* (London: Cassell and Co. 1891), p.44

33. Marcel Proust, *Swann's Way*, trans. C.K. Scott Moncrieff (New York: Modern Library, 1928), p.59

34. Tuan, p.230

35. Tuan, p.150

36. Tuan, p.28

37. Works consulted regarding the myth of Theseus and the Minotaur include the following:

Apollodorus, *The Library*, 2 vols. trans. James Frazer (London: William Heinemann, 1921)

Michael Ayrton, *The Maze Maker* (London: Longmans, green, and Co., 1967)

Ronald Burrows, *The Discoveries in Crete* (London: John Murray, 1908)

Diane De Turo Fortuna, "The Labyrinth of Art," Diss. Johns Hopkins Univ., 1967

Edith Hamilton, *Mythology* (New York: New American Library, 1942)

Ovidius, *Metamorphoses*, trans. Sir Samuel Garth (New York: Heritage Press, 1961)

Plutarch, *The Lives of the Nobel Grecians and Romans*, Vol.I, trans. Thomas North (Oxford: Basil Blackwell Press, 1928)

Louis Herbert, ed. *Mythology of All Races* (New York: Cooper Square Publishers, 1964)

38. Phillippe Borgeaud, "The Open Entrance to the Closed Palace of the King: The Greek Labyrinth in Context," *History of Religions*, 14 (August 1974), p.1-27. Also, S.H. Hooke, ed., *The Labyrinth: Further Studies in the Relations Between Myth and Ritual in the Ancient World* (New York: Macmillan, 1935), ix

39. C.N. Deedes, "The Labyrinth," in *The Labyrinth*, ed. S.H. Hooke, p.29

40. Deedes, p.42

41. Deedes, p.38

42. W.H. Matthews, *Mazes and Labyrinths: A General Account of Their History and Development* (London: Longmans, Green, and Co., 1922)

43. Mumford, p.10

44. Mumford, 56

45. Deedes, p.6

46. Paul Kuntz, "The Labyrinth," *Thought: A Review of Culture and Idea*, 47 (Spring 1972), p.11

47. Deedes, p.6]

48. Mumford, p.31

49. Georges Raillard, "L'Exemple," L'Emploi du Temps, Michel Butor (Paris: Minuit, 1957), p.487. "It is against this interest and this sad exclusion that Revel builds his tale." Translation by S. Muriel Tarr, CSA

50. Raillard, p.487

51. Charlotte Brontë, *Villette* (New York: Bigelow, Brown and Co., 1899), p.49

52. Philippe Aries, *Western Attitudes Toward Death: From the Middle Ages to the Present* (Baltimore: Johns Hopkins University Press, 1974), p.18

53. Georges Poulet, *The Metamorphoses of the Circle*, trans. Carley Dawson and Elliott Coleman (Baltimore: Johns Hopkins Press, 1961), p.49

54. Borgeaud, p.23

55. Kuntz, p.11

56. L.A. Murillo, "The Labyrinths of Jorge Luis Borges: An Introductory to the Stories of The Aleph," *Modern Language Quarterly* 20 (1959), p.266

2. *Villette:* An Irresolvable Tension

    Charlotte Brontë's exploration in *Villette* of the psychological trauma involved in a country girl's entry into adulthood takes the shape of a painful initiation into city living, an initiation only partially alleviated by the presence of church structures by which the protagonist tries to orient herself amidst urban confusion. The psychological conflict between Lucy Snow's remembrance of childhood innocence as well as interior atmosphere of "perpetual Sunday" (as she describes the religious nature of her Bretton recollection) is countered by her experience of death, orphanhood, and alienation as time and circumstance force her out of her childhood world and plunge her into the independence of adulthood, a movement that coincides with her move to two cities. Because Lucy does not cross the threshold between childhood and adulthood without looking back nostalgically and forward fearfully, her life is filled with ambiguities governed by her desire to maintain a childhood self-possession" and a simultaneous need "to taste life" as an adult.

    The dynamics of this tension are externalized in her response to church and city first in London and then in Villette. Subsequently, and by extension, when the church proves itself inadequate as a center of orientation joining Lucy psychologically to her childhood and extending its security, she turns her gaze inward on herself as a 'goddess' whose temple is externalized in Lucy's description of the moon as a church in the sky. The church as virginal sanctuary is opposed to the city which is for her a Babylon of confusion, disorientation, and license.

Fire and water, the city's elemental forces that consume and drown, are countered by her innate qualities of cold rationality and virginal purity, or coldness (Snowe) and light (Lucy). Initially Lucy turns to the institutional church as guardian of these qualities; but the church fails her by allowing peripheral dissipation to enter within its walls. Consequently, the moon in its own cold light becomes a temple to protect that self threatened by the city's penetrating fog and consuming fire, symbolic of death and corruption. But her fear of death and its concomitant refusal to become a citizen of either London or Villette is not simply a "universal" response. Instead, it grows from and takes place within the special context of nineteenth-century city and the forces which drive and mutilate it and its citizens. Lucy's strategy of mythologizing her identity, of turning to the timeless moon for value and protection, is clearly an evasion both of sexual maturity and of her historical environment.

The forces that compel Lucy to cling to the church even as she looks to the city for life, the image that attracts her to the church even as it is one of confinement, her desire for and yet fear of the city --- these are the ambiguities that characterize the psychological labyrinth in which Lucy finds herself, a labyrinth reproduced topographically in the tension between church and city, center and periphery.

After briefly giving an account of childhood bliss in a country setting, Lucy Snowe concludes her early reminiscence with her recollection of natural tragedy, the inscrutable finality of which sends her in pursuit of the city idealized as God's dwelling among men, where He will wipe every tear from their eyes. Influenced by a Biblical and Bunyanesque glorification of the city as a type of heaven on earth, Lucy anticipates her departure from the countryside and what she calls the "rust of obscurity": "I mentally saw within reach what I had never beheld with my bodily eyes: I saw London."[1] The tone of expectancy and faith in Lucy's diction echoes the Apostle's apocalyptic account: "I saw the holy city, and the new Jerusalem," he records, "coming down from God out of heaven" (Rev. 21:2). Such idealizing corresponds to Charlotte Brontë's own childhood conception of the city, when "after the first reading of *Pilgrim's Progress* and hearing constantly from the servants what a fine town Bradford was, she set off quite alone to find it." Similarly, when "she read of Paris as a little girl, she felt that she must see it 'or perish'."[2] As it had been for her creator, then, in the days of her youth, Lucy's hope of finding a lasting dwelling place, friendship, security, all life's gifts of which she has suddenly and irrevocably been deprived in the country, lies in the city.

Although Lucy has experienced security, protection, and household order provided by religion's calming influence, that experience has been a fleeting one. Having only tasted life's promise, Lucy is suddenly robbed of family, home, and financial security when nature's inscrutable law shows its power by taking the lives of her whole family as well as that of her only employer and companion. In describing the experience that turns her gaze toward the city, Lucy speaks of death metaphorically as a drowning experience: "The ship was lost, the crew perished" (36). Moreover, Ms. Marchmont's solitary life and lonely death give added impetus to Lucy's desire to seek a life in the city, for she receives from them a premonition of her own possible future should she choose to remain in the country. Orphaned and destitute, Lucy naturally turns to the city. For the country, in spite of its seeming promise to remain always like "the gliding of a full river through a plain," (2) suddenly had revealed its hidden potential as a swelling "heavy tempest" (36) that has swallowed her entire family in death, leaving her without even the means of physical survival. Her hope, therefore, takes the shape of London. As the sun clears away the fog and night on that first morning in the city, Lucy records concerning herself that her heart "grew as quickly as Jonah's gourd" (52). Like its Biblical prototype, however, for which "God arranged that a worm" (Jonah 4:5-8) should smite and wither it, Lucy's heart will also wither as suddenly.

The tension between church and city which Lucy experiences in London serves to externalize her psychological inability to bridge the gap between a subconscious desire to regain childhood security and her simultaneous need for adult independence, her fear of death and her simultaneous desire to taste life. Like the cathedral that is self-contained and enclosed "above [her] head, above the house-tops, co-elevate almost with the clouds" (54), Lucy inhabits the city physically but keeps herself psychologically aloof from it. In this way, Charlotte Brontë dramatizes Lucy's position on the horns of a dilemma: Psychologically Lucy is torn between the city's call to self-surrender and childhood's clinging to self-preservation. To use Lucy's comparison when describing her response to the death of her family, she fears falling overboard, the horror of "the rush and saltness of briny waves in [her] throat, and their icy pressure on [her] lungs" (36). Enclosed within the dome of St. Paul's Lucy is figuratively above the flood that threatens to swallow her when walking the city streets. London from above, like Bretton from her godmother's balcony, takes on the calming aspect of order. While the dome gives Lucy a sense of power and security from the city's confusion, it does not satisfy her need for psychological grown and adult stimulation. At the same time, however, Lucy recognizes the city to be a place beneficial to psychological growth, exposure, stimulation, adventure, and knowledge.

As a result, Lucy is both attracted to London and frightened by it. She feels calm only when covered by the cathedral's shadow or enclosed within its dome. Like the balcony of her godmother's home, the dome gives Lucy the advantage of observing without being observed in turn. Typified by the church whose architecture overshadows the city without participating in its confusion, Lucy beholds London without incurring the vulnerability that comes with direct involvement. Consequently, she overlooks being overcharged by waiters and treated condescendingly by porters in the boarding house where she has a room.

Why Lucy glorifies the city from a distance, but avoids direct participation in it when there, can be explained by her subconscious fear of death, which is manifested rather than overcome by the city as she had hoped. Both Biblical City of God and Bunyanesque Celestial City are holy because there God's chosen ones will triumph over the forces of time and death. In its architecture, the church symbolized this triumphant city. The dome represented the vault of heaven, while the floor signified the earth. In its vertical dimension the dome captured a sense of transcendence, while its horizontal aspect indicated the participation of temporality in eternity. Lucy's response to the church in the city, accordingly, has little to do with its doctrinal teaching or social involvement. As she confesses at one point, constancy of heart must be of greater value to God than "the just motion of satellites about their planets, of planets about their suns, of suns around that mighty unseen centre incomprehensible" (506). Consequently, it is St. Paul's architectural transcendence and its symbolic dominance over the city's transitory confusion that appeals to Lucy: "I saw a solemn, orbed mass, dark blue and dim--THE DOME," she writes (52). The boldface type and capital letters by which she isolates and emphasizes the word indicate the dome's centrality for her in defining the city. As a nineteenth century heroine, Lucy might naturally be awed by the sight of London's cathedral, since the status of the title 'city' was ordinarily reserved for those towns that could boast possession of a cathedral.[3]

For Lucy, the City of God remains symbolically then only in the cathedral. Otherwise, London threatens loss of self-identity, a psychological death. Although she gradually gets excited by the city, "its business, its rush, its roar" (53), and expresses her desire "to taste life" (53) in its fullness here, Lucy's first and last impressions of London are of it as a watery grave, from the "dark, raw, and rainy" (4) atmosphere that greets her to its inky black river that carries her away shortly thereafter. Although Lucy congratulates herself for the prodigious "amount of life" she has lived in her one and only morning stroll through London's streets, she is really no more than a sightseer in what she calls "the heart of the city" (53. Like the poet who verbally pictured life as a giant seething beneath an enchanted castle, Lucy perceives death lurking in the waters whose surface mirrors the city.[4] The river is black "as a torrent of ink" and on its face Lucy sees a reflection of the city's own face. The image that comes to her mind is that "of the Styx, and of Charon rowing some solitary soul to the land of Shades" (55).

Although Lucy occasionally ventures beyond the boarding school walls into the city with its geographical expanse and multifarious forms of life, she fears severing the cord that binds her psychologically to the security of her Bretton past. What if London is no more than a

Slough of Despond, "the product of the pride and vanity which causes men to cling to a life that remains erratic and purposeless."⁵ Speaking like one trapped in a mental if not a physical labyrinth, Lucy expresses her bewilderment in Bunyanesque terms:

> What was I doing here alone in great London? What should I do on the morrow? What prospects had I in life? What friends had I on earth? Whence did I come? Whither should I go? What should I do? (50)

After a brief mental struggle, evidenced by the tears on her pillow that first night in London, Lucy feels confident that, even if she is lost in a labyrinth that is physical as well as psychological, there is a direction that will eventually yield a center if she will only advance and not try to retreat. Consequently, she writes, "I had a strong, vague persuasion that it was better to go forward than backward" (51) and that she was indeed going forward. Authority providing direction for her future is the hope upon which Lucy bases her continued quest through this city she calls "a Babylon and a wilderness," a place that threatens her "powers of clear thought and steady self-possession" (50).

Lucy's London experience is a brief one and the city itself soon left behind never to be revisited; nevertheless, the episode itself captures in cursory fashion the dynamic of Lucy's initial response to Villette as one of fear which draws her to its religious center as a way of psychological as well as physical escape.⁶ Because the city originally received its psychological and architectural orientation from its centrally located church, it is significant that Villette's former convent, although still located at the heart of the city, is now only a boarding school. Religious ideals no longer hold; education, once the handmaid of spirituality, is now its mistress. While St. Paul's retains its original status as a cathedral whose architectural prominence overshadows the city, and while the city's atmosphere suggests death only in general terms, Villette's center endorses the deadening strictures of a convent enclosure without retaining its original, life-giving spirit.

Here it may be interesting to note that Dickens in *Edwin Drood* moves to a provincial city to get the pure revulsion of holy buildings perverted. London for both writers may be corrupt, but it is vital. The atmosphere of Villette's streets suggests more poignantly than does London's the city's threat to Lucy's psychological integrity. Because she is no longer a child, but is reluctant to surrender the security once briefly experienced as a child, Lucy fears the city and idolizes the guide who directs her to its convent-related enclosure.

Like London, but with added emphasis and dimension, the city of Villette is a kind of watery grave in its dark, wet atmosphere made more threatening by two men who pursue her through the city's dark, wet streets until she gets lost in running from them. Water alone is an image sufficient to suggest physical death to Lucy, who describes the loss of her family as a drowning experience. Villette, however, has a particularly ominous death-like quality in its "thick fog and small dense rain---darkness, that might almost be felt" (67), which has settled on the city when Lucy arrives.

Added to Lucy's fear of getting lost physically, a getting lost that reflects psychological disintegration as well, is Lucy's fear of losing her integrity through loss of virginal innocence. As in the mythic labyrinth, so too in the city, the sacrifice of virginity is coupled with physical and psychological disorientation. Lost and alone in Villette as in London, Lucy walks a labyrinthine path that is both "miry" and "black as midnight" (70) among trees dripping water. While the shadow of St. Paul's functions symbolically as a psychological glass bubble under which Lucy is shielded from self-disclosure, Villette's penetrating rain and darkness prefigure the violation of her person, a violation avoided in London by the cathedral that gave her a sense of being in and yet not of the city. Here, instead of feeling herself secure within the shadow of St. Paul's, Lucy experiences herself within the shadow of sinister men in pursuit of her. Fearful of losing her sense of self-possession as she is, Lucy regards this supposed threat to her virginal integrity as an assault on her entire well-being. Unburdening herself of the nightmare in written reflection, Lucy confesses: "Puzzled, out of breath, all my pulses throbbing in inevitable agitation, I knew not where to turn" (71).

As in London when questions of where to go and what to do plagued her, so too in Villette, Lucy subconsciously seeks an authoritative image in a church structure. Just as she anticipated comfort even at a distance in the assurance that she lay in the shadow of St. Paul's, so too does she experience initial relief in her chance discovery of the ancient convent at the heart of Villette. Significant in relation to the framework of the myth of Theseus and the labyrinth, Lucy is greeted in this city by one she regards as a stranger, who provides her with the thread of verbal directions that eventually takes her to shelter at the very heart of Villette. Though they fail to recognize each other as former companions in the Bretton household, Lucy expresses an intuitive trust in the helper provided to her: "In the double gloom of trees and fog, I could not see my guide: I could only follow his tread. Not the least fear had I: I believe I would have followed that frank tread through continual night, to the world's end" (70). It is John Bretton, a thread uniting her to that happy past, who guides her into the house of that "Minos in petticoats" who directs her future. As a matter of fact, the Rue Fossette is much like a nursery, at first glance a promise of security under the care of a godmother figure; in short it is a symbolic return to a guarded childhood.

In its very name Villette promises the expansive freedom of a city (ville) and the diminutive, enclosing character of a village (-ette). In truth, the boarding school on the Rue Fossette returns Lucy psychologically to the safe and secure world of Bretton even though it is located at the very core of the metropolis. Describing her first impressions, Lucy cites its diminutive qualities, like the sleeping quarters which "were the queerest little dormitories," having once been nuns' cells. Lucy also takes mental note of three children asleep in "three tiny beds" (76). The boarders are elsewhere called infants, and Lucy occupies the "watchtower of the nursery"(85). It is to this watchtower that Lucy later retreats whenever she feels her privacy violated. For her the watchtower and later the attic are private sanctuaries within Villette comparable to St. Paul's in affording her the privacy to withdraw into herself, to retreat from the city's threatening encroachments. As in London, she is once again both architecturally and psychologically lifted out of the confusion involved in the business of living represented by the city. Just as Lucy always wears drab colors (so that she cannot even recognize herself in the mirror when forced to wear flashy pink), so too, she finds the convent's secluded areas more suited to herself than the city's exterior facade. When alone, Lucy is free from subjection to or possession by others; but when among urban society, she fears losing touch with herself and her essential simplicity in the forced guise of pretentious sophistication. The day when she is compelled to leave the "watchtower of the nursery" and "the enchantment of distance" provided by it is a sad one for Lucy, who fears "intercourse" with the world (85).

On the other hand, however, Lucy states her preference for city in opposition to country living, her desire for recognition in contrast to obscurity. The museum episode is a telling one in dramatizing the tightrope Lucy mentally walks between the city's offer to expand her knowledge and the church's simultaneous call to preserve original innocence. The contrast is personified in the opposing viewpoints of the urbanized John and the ministerial Paul, her guides through the museum's art gallery. While John gazes unabashedly upon the practically nude "Cleopatra" lounging in a risque posture, Paul shields himself and the virginal Lucy from it by directing her attention to a grouping of domestic scenes. For an audience of Charlotte Brontë's time, portraits of nude, oriental queens like Cleopatra typified a mother goddess who enslaved men to her whims by means of her seductive arts. Moreover, such queens embodied the qualities of restlessness, perpetual dissatisfaction, and complete lack of restraint.[7] Lucy later invokes the moon goddess as her votary. Now she submits to M. Paul's direction in surrounding herself with images of enclosure rather than exposure.

Like the ambiguity within Lucy between her longing to experience life and her simultaneous fear of compromising her innocence, there is a like ambiguity in John which attracts her to him even though he is a man of the city she fears. In one sense, she can satisfy her longing to "taste life" by mentally enclosing herself within his extroverted personality. Consequently she imagines his personality segmented into compartments with all of his worldly acquaintances and enterprises separated from one special "little closet over the door of which is written 'Lucy's Room'." On the other hand, however, she imagines herself as a refuge for John, a "tabernacle for a host" (548) in that she preserves within herself their common link with an Edenic past. In likening him to "the gold image" of Nebuchadnezzar, Lucy idolizes his preservation of innate goodness in the midst of worldly temptation. Lucy's veneration of John is indicated by her trust that in the "goodly mansion, his heart, he kept one little place under the skylights where Lucy might have entertainment"(548). In John's company, Lucy can witness the city's dangerous excitement without surrendering herself to it. Lucy's visits to the museum of fine art discussed above and to the theater discussed later are examples of temptation through which John passes unscathed. John is the adult Lucy would like to be by proxy.

An example of John's ability to transport Lucy back to childhood as well, is exemplified in the chapter regarding Lucy's illness. In a kind of wish-fulfillment episode, childhood associations with John Bretton, and the convent enclosure are all brought together in a scene that resembles a dream more than reality. Having collapsed in a faint on the streets of Villette, Lucy recounts coming out of a state of delirium into a vision too comfortingly familiar to be real. It was like walking to "'auld lang syne,'" which "smiled out of every nook" (195), she recalls. Her eye also takes in the diminutive, that quality of the convent that first appeals to her in its association with childhood. She takes special note of "two oval miniatures over the mantelpiece," and on the mantel "two china vases, some relic of a diminutive tea-service" (195). Such retreat, however, is dangerous, just as Nebuchadnezzar was dangerously worshipping a false god, an insight Charlotte Brontë withholds from Lucy, who yields to the comfort of being nursed like a child. There is more than writing on the wall in the flowered wallpaper Lucy describes: "A slight but endless garland of azure forget-me-nots ran mazed and bewildered amongst gold leaves and tendrils" (194).

Subtly introduced, the image can be interpreted as a figure of Lucy's psychological state. The forget-me-nots are her treasured childhood memories. Slight but endless, the garland is the childhood she carries with her psychologically even though it has vanished temporally. The flowers' mazed and bewildered condition reflects her general state of mind, which believes it is "better to go forward than backward" (51), but fears the loss of pristine virtue (gold leaves) amidst the snares of experience (tendrils) involved in pushing forward into adulthood. As much as she wishes it were not, Bretton is a bygone phase in her life, not a still point to which she can return at will or remain indefinitely in once recovered. Spatially as well as temporally, the Bretton household has been incorporated into Villette; for Lucy explains that although she wakes to a vision of the old Bretton household, that home is now located within Villette. Village life has been incorporated into the city.

Symbolically, the labyrinth too, encompasses a world larger than the enclosure of childhood. In the large world of adulthood, Lucy subconsciously defines her own center in terms of self-possession as a virtue to be preserved and guarded rather than a quality to be acquired through growth in experience. Consequently, in St. Paul's, the Rue Fossette, and her return to Villette's Bretton household, Lucy continuously tests each experience not for what she may have gained, but for what she has been able to preserve. Always fearful of the city as a passion pit, Lucy emulates the clear logic by which Count Bassom-Pierre, gracious mediator between the little world of Bretton and the great world of business enterprise beyond, orders his life. Lucy's reflection reveals her estimation of his outlook: "Once having seized the thread, it had guided him through a long labyrinth" (506).

Again, however, Lucy rests on the horns of a dilemma; for an unspoken assumption, but one on which Lucy acts, is that there exists an institutional authority by which life is to be directed, an authority that will reenforce what she innately believes. Consequently, she never wholly abandons either church or city, even though they fail to satisfy her need for order and direction.

It is to the city that she looks for the thread that will guide her along the path of reason to a haven of order, and the assurance, not only of human, but of divine sponsorship as well. But the city itself is divided between its religious center and its secular periphery. While the former is too restrictive, the latter is too permissive. Lucy inhabits the labyrinthine city whose periphery contains temptation in the person of Vashti, the erotic dancer, and whose center encloses imposed restraint in the person of Madame Beck. Vashti personifies Lucy's desire to reach out, explore, dare the unknown and demonic, while Madame Beck embodies restraint, order, and the safety of defined limits.

Lucy's impression of Vashti, the very embodiment of the city in her unrestrained movements, is that of death draped in crimson. Like the water of her childhood that drowns, Vashti is the fire that consumes. Though opposed as contraries, both are equally destructive of life and order. Framing the Vashti dance scene are the ghostly apparition of a nun buried alive for violating her vow of chastity, and the conflagration of the theater itself. Passion and its danger are thus associated with fire, death, and the demonic. Passion, like fire, is deadly in its power "to bring all of life to its conclusion, to its hereafter."[8]

Appropriately, Vashti, already burned out emotionally on stage by the end of her performance, is also physically dead, as Lucy takes care to note, when she pens her reminiscence of the event. Like fire, whose effect on its object is so deep, swift, and definite, Lucy's response is one of horror as well as marvel: "It was a marvelous sight; a mighty vision. It was a spectacle low, horrible, immoral" (306). While she is fascinated, Lucy ultimately turns her gaze toward John from whom she receives the assurance that order will be re-established; for he is a "cool, young Briton" (308). Later Lucy will turn her gaze toward the moon for its possession of this same quality -- cool radiance.

In contrast to the passionate Vashti stands the calculating Madame Beck. As guardian of the enclosure on the Rue Fossette, she makes the rules and oversees their execution. In Lucy's judgment, Madame Beck is "the right sort of Minos in petticoats"(81). A demi-god like the Minos of myth who sacrificed virgins to the Minotaur, Madame

Beck maintains a house of virgins dedicated to the worship of the Christian divinity. Although the boarding school is no longer a convent, Madame Beck enforces the observance of a daily horarium that includes spiritual reading, common prayer, and the rules of the cloister, no men being admitted except by special dispensation.

Yet even in this virginal cloister so rigidly guarded, Lucy must contend with sexual impulses, whose power to destroy resembles that of fire or water. Having fled from the city's attempt to drown her in its water and consume her in its flames, Lucy discovers rats within the enclosure itself. As surely as fire and water, rats symbolize Lucy's terror of destruction and violation. Locked in the attic to rehearse her lines for a play, Lucy describes seeing "a very dark and large rat, with a long tail" that comes "gliding out from the squalid alcove" (157), compelling her to gather her dress about her and leap onto a chest. Clearly suggesting by this reaction that Lucy's fear is sexually motivated, Charlotte Brontë demonstrates Lucy's vulnerability to nature's law of change (synonymous here with a fall from original innocence or grace) whether she yield to passion or discipline her conduct by reason.

Even here in the attic, this place consecrated by Lucy as her solitary retreat, the fragility of her maidenhood is threatened by forces beyond her power to control, the natural forces of change working within her very person. In this case that natural force is sexual maturation, a death to childhood and an entry into adulthood.

The suggestion of sexual violation indicated by Lucy's response to the rat is made more explicit by the appearance of the nun who, according to legend, was buried alive for violating her vow of chastity. In the garden where the nun is supposedly interred, Lucy later buries the letter initially magnified in her mind as a love letter. This act of burying is symbolic of her desire to bury the desires of the flesh as well, desires associated with the city's full-fleshed Cleopatra and passionate Vashti. Madame Beck is indeed a "Minos in petticoats," who imprisons virgins only to prepare them for the sacrifice in which their virginity will be lost. For in a real sense, the boarding school is a prelude to courtship and marriage. In spite of the rules, an occasional *billet doux* gets tossed over the wall, and dances are held to which men are invited. In short, the demonic forces of change, revealed by the capriciousness of passion and sexuality in the city, have penetrated its once consecrated enclosure as well. The convent can only lessen the impact of time's inevitable movement away from childhood innocence, rather than stop that process. Neither can Lucy hinder nature's law operating within herself.

The contrast between city and convent, sexuality and virginity, is personified in that between the apostle and prophet after whom Charlotte Brontë may have named John Bretton and M. Paul. St. Paul is the Christian ascetic who preached chastity as the better way: "In other words," he wrote in his Letter to the Corinthians, "the man who sees that his daughter is married has done a good thing, but the man who keeps his daughter unmarried has done something better" (I Cor. 7:38). The glorified, spiritual Christ was the subject of his teaching.

Conversely, St. John the Baptist announced Christ's coming in the flesh, thereby reaffirming the body's essential dignity. Appropriately, John Bretton is a doctor dedicated to physical healing. Subconsciously, Lucy fears her sexuality, tied to mortality as it is, even as she fears and yet occasionally yields to her desire for the city's material body. John, at home in the city himself, functions as Lucy's guide there. In his presence, she observes what she calls its immorality without being tainted by it herself. In the midst of the burning theater, for example, John's healing power allays even fire's destructive force. Without her childhood companion at her side, however, Lucy experiences only alienation and danger in the city. Paul, on the other hand, guides her through realms of intellectual and spiritual discipline and devotion.

The womb-like dome of St. Paul's, which preaches in stone the apostle Paul's message of a spiritual life of interior devotion, is countered by the steeple of St. Jean Baptiste, whose architecture signifies a reaching out, a lifting out of confinement and limitation.

In the end, however, union is established with neither John nor Paul, though Paul is the more promising candidate; for in spite of her need to embrace either self-surrender in the city or self-denial in the convent, Lucy is able to do neither. Instead, she moves from enclosure to enclosure in her fear of losing the little self-identity acquired in the Bretton household.

If London constitutes a venture of guarded ascent from private sitting room to church dome, Villette comprises a guarded descent from convent attic to garden. For when the convent attic, with its once protective maze of hanging drapery, piled lumber, and cobwebs, is invaded by rats, prying eyes, and the ghostly apparition, Lucy seeks the garden enclosure, much as she retreats to the convent when the city threatens her quiet composure: "This garden, in a city-heart, lay still as a houseless wild."9

Walled in by shrubbery on both sides of the garden walk with a canopy of foliage overhead, Lucy makes for herself a hermitage protected from human intrusion by natural vegetation. Contrary to city, church, and untamed nature, the garden is a place set apart where all is ordered and delimited without making any demands on its devotee. Neither self-surrender nor self-denial is required of its votary. In accord with this retreat, Lucy is herself a hermitess afraid to surrender to either city or church, as both have betrayed their inability to protect her from the forces of destruction and death.

Although she speaks in the third person masculine, Lucy is rationalizing about her own fears when she soliloquizes of the hermit who

> if he be sensible, he will swallow his own thoughts, and lock up his own emotions during these weeks of inward winter. He will know that Destiny designed him to imitate, on occasion, the dormouse, and he will be conformable: make a tidy ball of himself, creep into a hole of life's wall, and submit decently to the drift which blows in and soon blocks him up, preserving him in ice for the season (317).

Such is the character of Lucy Snowe as her very name implies. Neither city nor church is successful in breaking the barrier of ice she has erected around herself. Even as a child, Lucy preferred to repress emotion's warmth, considering its expression an act of weakness. Observing Paulina's emotional nature, Lucy judges her destined for a life of instability and capriciousness.

Convinced that reason is better than passion, ice preferable to fire, and retreat better than entanglement, Lucy understandably pays homage to the moon.[10] Not without imaginative resources, Lucy builds for herself a sacred space in the sky. The moon is envisioned as an imaginary church, an objective correlative for the self she desires to be --all-encompassing and yet aloof, bright as fire and yet pure as light. In adulation, she exclaims:

> To thee neither hands build, nor lips consecrate: but hearts, through ages, are faithful to thy worship. A dwelling thou hast, too wide for walls, too high for dome--a temple whose floors are space--rites whose mysteries transpire in presence, to the kindling, the harmony of worlds! (272)

Like the dome of St. Paul's and the enclosure on the Rue Fossette, the moon comforts in that it lifts her spirit out of present confusion and returns her in memory to childhood. The moon as a globe-enclosing crescent leaning against a spire recalls a scene of this same moon leaning against an old thorn tree:

> A moon was in the sky, not a full moon, but a young crescent. I saw her through a space in the boughs overhead. She and the stars, visible beside her, were no strangers where all else was strange: my childhood knew them. I had seen that golden sign with the dark globe in its curve leaning back on azure, beside an old thorn at the top of an old field, in Old England, in long past day; just as it now leaned back beside a stately spire in this continental capital (126).

Invoked as a "young crescent," the moon is associated with Artemis, chaste goddess of the chase, who, by vowing eternal virginity, remains ever young as patroness of children. In contrast to Hecate, goddess of the waning moon, and as such, goddess of bewitching change and of the fickle, Artemis is ever new, never-changing. Of the latter Lucy is a worthy devotee.

But Artemis is even more than maiden eternally young, she is also androgynous. With her hunting tunic and silver bow (symbolic of the crescent moon), Artemis fulfills a masculine role as goddess of the hunt. Uniting masculinity and femininity within a single nature, Artemis is complete within herself.[11] Lucy, too, yearns for this sense of wholeness signified by androgyny. Given a male role in a play that allows her to act the part of the man while remaining a woman, she acknowledges: "I had consented to take a man's name and part," but "would keep my own dress" (161). Playing a man's role, she can safely eclipse with her own borrowed masculine light the lesser flirtatious shafts of her female rival on stage. And yet, as a woman in reality, she can use her disguise to flirt boldly and without fear of detection with the man in the audience whose attention she desires.

Recalling that play at a later date, Lucy writes: "What I felt that night, and what I did, I no more expected to feel and do than to be lifted in a trance to the seventh heaven" (165). For a brief moment limits are transgressed as she acts the part of male aggressiveness and yet secretly acknowledges her feminine reserve, which forbids openly admitting her dependence.

Off-stage, Lucy finds herself accusing her classmates of just such aggressive behavior in seeking the city merely as a mating place. Publicly, therefore, she excludes herself from their company, but privately she longs to participate in such escapades herself. Like the chaste Artemis, who punishes violators against chastity, Lucy judges with particular harshness Ginevre's flirtatious nature. In the same way, she finds fault with the man who violates the sanctuary of the enclosure by tossing the love letter over the wall even as she secretly hopes it might be addressed to herself.

Artemis, goddess of the crescent or virgin moon, is the divinity Lucy adopts as her own. Seen from the garden of the convent, which is located geographically at the center of labyrinthine Villette and supervised by its Minos, Madame Beck, the crescent moon is suggestive of its mythic representation in the *labyrs* or double-headed axe, "a familiar emblem of Cretin sovereignty--shaped like a waxing and a waning moon joined together back to back, and symbolizing the creative as well as the destructive power of the goddess."[12]

Identifying herself with the waxing phase of the moon, Lucy looks back to her childhood, when, in fact, time is carrying her inevitably toward its waning or Hecate phase. She dreams of Edenic youth while her fate in old age is being decided for her. She continues to look to the past in her temptation to make of it through John "a golden image" (113) and a "tabernacle for a host" (548) while M. Paul plans her future for her.

The home Paul secures for her in the Faubourg Clotilde comes as a complete surprise to her. Like the waning moon which is easily mistaken for a waxing one, Lucy characteristically views this home in light of the past rather than the future. Enjoying a moonlight stroll with M. Paul from this new home on the Faubourg back to the boarding school on the Rue Fossette, Lucy reads a retrospective message in the moon:

> We walked back to the Rue Fossette by moonlight--such moonlight as fell on Eden--shining through the shades of the Great Garden, and haply gilding a path glorious for a step divine--a Presence nameless. Once in their lives some men and women go back to these first fresh days of our great Sire and Mother--taste that grand morning's dew--bathe in its sunrise (589).

She may believe she is moving forward, but her reflection suggests the past, an Edenic past. Although she rejoices in this gift from M. Paul, the home itself is actually a Bretton-like cluster of "nooks" in a "nutshell" (582). And behind this little home is a garden complete with "a pale statue [that] leaned over the place of waters" of a fountain that rings a "lulling vesper) (585). The description suggests the atmosphere of her former convent enclosure. Whatever name it may bear, Lucy's new home is a retreat transferred from the center to the boundary between city and country, a miniature center that comfortably orders her horizons rather than court with urban demons.

Although this new boarding school in the Faubourg Clotilde is within the city limits, its prospect includes country fields. Moreover, Clotilde, its namesake and patroness of maiden warriors, serves as the Christian counterpart of Artemis with her characteristic symbols the bow and arrow.[13] In leaving the Rue Fossette ('little grave') Lucy enters the faubourg, an "imitation" or "sham" city, a "faux," as "faubourg" is commonly translated in French folk etymology.[14] In a sense, Lucy's new home is merely an imitation of the old center moved to the boundary between city and country. This sham Rue Fossette comes as close as possible to leaving both city and church without actually doing either. Departing from the "little grave" prepared by madame Minos for marriage's future sacrificial victims, Lucy dreams of perpetuating her youth as the protectress of children, a title belonging to the moon goddess herself. Eternal virginity, the request of Artemis at the age of three, will also be Lucy's fate if M. Paul is indeed lost at sea as Charlotte Brontë intimates.[15] Unable to resolve the tensions that govern her life, "Lucy ends as she began, estranged by shipwreck from her one possible home."[16] In the words of a twentieth century critic, "she is fixed in the pale virgin crescent, though she loves two men."[17]

References to moonlight in conjunction with Lucy's childhood and convent experience define her response to the city as well. Looking at the Cleopatra portrait in the museum and attending the Vashti dance enkindle fires within Lucy that are externalized in those that consume the theater. The moon's fire, on the other hand, is cold. Its light is a calming one, greater than the glories of the city. A brief enchantment with the city's splendor is followed by a persistent search for the cooling influence of a moon-embossed pond. Enchantment grips her when midnight reveals the city park in a blaze of light, dancing, and festivity:

> Villette is one blaze, one broad illumination; the whole world seems a road; moonlight and heavens are banished;the town, by her own flambeaux, beholds her own splendor--gay dresses, grand equipages, fine horses and gallant riders throng the bright streets . . . (542).

For a moment the city is an earthly replica of the celestial order, shining by its own light like Isaiah's holy city, the new Jerusalem, rather than the borrowed light of the moon; "No more will the sun give daylight, nor moonlight shine on you, but Yahweh will be your everlasting light, your God will be your splendor" (Is.60:19). Entering into the city's festivity, Lucy finds herself "plunged amidst a gay, living, joyous crowd" (542).

In her state of enchantment, Lucy sees the park as representing the best of both church and city. Nature is preserved here, but it is a cultivated, ordered nature as in the convent garden; and the city is an architectural paradise, a sacred place, in its transcendent thrust heavenward:

> In a land of enchantment, a garden most gorgeous, a plain sprinkled with colored meteors, a forest with sparks of purple and ruby and golden fire gemming the foliage; a region, not of trees and shadow, but of strangest architectural wealth--of altar and of temple, of pyramid, obelisk, and sphinx; incredible to say, the wonders and the symbols of Egypt teemed throughout the park of Villette (543).

The city, like John's mystic vision of the heavenly Jerusalem, glitters "like some precious jewel . . . " (Rev.21:12). It is also Isaiah's vision of the new Jerusalem: "Unhappy creature, storm-tossed, disconsolate," Isaiah speaks in the name of the Lord of this city, "I will make rubies your battlements, your gates crystal, and your entire wall precious stones" (Is.54:11-12). Moreover, the ancient burial ground as foundation of church and city is contained here in Villette's park where "the sacred bones of martyrs" (543) consecrate the city celebration.

The impression of the city as sacred is only fleeting, however, inspired as it is by Lucy's state of enchantment, which is always ephemeral by nature. After a brief observation, she finds herself attracted, as by a magnet, to the park's circular basin. "My vague aim, as I went," she admits,

> was to find the stone-basin, with its center: clear depth and green lining: of that coolness and verdure I thought, with the passionate thirst of unconscious fever. Amidst the glare, and hurry, and throng, and noise, I still secretly and chiefly longed to come on that circular mirror of crystal, and surprise the moon glassing therein her pearly front (544).

Once again her refuge is the moon. In the midst of the glittering, mulling crowds, Lucy herself pursues this center with its moon in "glory and silence" triumphant (562). The church gives meaning to the festivity of the city, it having been sanctioned with "a solemn Te Deum in St. Jean Baptiste," but the moon gives meaning to Lucy's presence there. The attitude is already struck in a poem of Charlotte's published in 1846:

> Above the city hung the moon
> Right o'er a plot of ground
> Where flowers and orchard-trees are fenced
> With lofty walls around.[18]

The moon imparts to a garden enclosed that sense of completeness which is both attitudinal and imagistic. The park as center of city celebration would itself have been a mere "show of Vanity Fair had not Lucy discovered its presiding goddess. On another occasion Lucy reflects: "Where indeed, does the moon not look well? What is the scene, confined or expansive, which her orb does not hallow?" (562) Regarding the significance of the moon in relation to Lucy, a critic has put it succinctly by saying that it "could hallow a scene, be a comrade, exert an influence, supply strength, echo a great myth, and suggest the presence of the divine."[19] Only when Lucy beholds the moon itself or its reflected face does she experience calm in the midst of city turbulence.

As Lucy makes her way through city streets back to the Rue Fossette after the festival, she is guided by moonlight rather than John or M. Paul. She feels at peace under its sway. Speaking of the spent city she is leaving behind, Lucy notes: "Drum, trumpet, bugle, had uttered their clangour, and were forgotten; with pencil ray she [the moon] wrote on heaven and earth records for archives everlasting (562). Where all else is passing, the moon reigns everlasting, "unchangeable in the heavens," as the psalmist phrases it.

The moon as symbol of celestial order which transcends the vagaries of time and place serves as Lucy's alternative for a bewildering city and a confining church. Left alone when the long vacation takes all other boarders away, Lucy soon rushes out into the streets desperately in need of social communion. Finding no solace in the passing strangers, she wanders into a church and its confessional. Although the experience gives momentary relief, it ends in Lucy's vision of herself confined in a cloistered convent counting her beads. Freed from the Babylonian wilderness of city streets, Lucy imagines herself in danger of confinement in a "Babylonish furnace" (191).

The moon's cool light calms Lucy's troubled spirit at night, but she must learn to live in a daylight world. Often, therefore, it is the sound of the church bell that orients her in a world of temporality and caprice. Historically, the distance which the sound of the church bell carried determined the city's limits. For Lucy, the bells define limits and inspire meditative reflection on events just ended or about to begin. During her first days on the Rue Fossette, for example, Lucy notes the "sunset or the hour of salut" by the sound of "the bells of St. Jean Baptiste" that "peal out with their sweet, soft, exalted sound" (123). The sound of the church bells gives her comfort here as formerly in London, where she was lulled to sleep by the sound of the bell's "deep, low mighty tone" (151). Bells provide a sense of temporal order.

Those bells also serve as a witness to secure the hour in which Lucy discovers the *billet-doux* tossed over the garden wall: "Nine was striking by St. Jean Baptiste's clock: day was fading, but it was not dark" (127). the hour is important, approaching the limit of day as it is, just as the letter threatens encroachment into the convent walls. Lucy measures the time and intensity of her daydreaming by the same church bell: "By the clock of St. Jean Baptiste, that dream remained scarce fifteen minutes--a brief space, but sufficing to wring my whole frame with unknown anguish" (187), she confides. John Bretton, whose affection she desires but is afraid to seek openly because of her inferiority complex, causes this anguish by his failure to perceive, let alone fulfill, this need to be loved which she herself seems consciously to deny.

The nun-like Lucy suppresses these feelings as a weakness, glad for the bells that wake her out of such revery. Like the legendary nun buried alive for violating the limits set by her vow, Lucy is buried psychologically *dans une fossette* in her fear that she too might violate some duty in openly seeking love: "'Leave your souls to me,'" she hears the church whispering, "I hold their cure . . . guide their course." Such is the voice Lucy hears within, and which the church bell echoes without. Limits being approached or violated characterize all the moments in which Lucy hears them.

Other church bells guide Lucy when she ventures beyond hearing distance of St. Jean Baptiste. Sent on a mission into an unknown part of the city on behalf of Madame Beck, Lucy hears and mentally notes "an unknown clock from an unknown tower (St. Jean Baptiste's voice was not too distant to be audible) . . . tolling the third quarter past five" (462). Having ventured beyond familiar territory, Lucy has physically passed beyond a limit. More importantly, however, she is about to transgress a psychological one. Duped by Madame Walraven's intentionally misleading account of Paul's continued attachment to a lost love, Lucy is consequently led to lose hope in his ever being able to love her. Unworthy and afraid of a physical relationship with John, Lucy believes herself shut out from the possibility of even a spiritual love relationship with M. Paul, his spiritual love devoted to a bride of the church taken from him in death. Only after much needless suffering does Lucy learn the truth.

Characteristically, Lucy hears church bells at the sunset hour or after. Although Lucy welcomes the nocturnal moon "as the source of the ability to advance, of power and strength,"[20] she similarly heeds the bells which allay the city's daylight commotion. The peal of the bells of St. Jean Baptiste sound to her ear only when "the broad, vulgar middle of the day" has subsided. Lucy hears the bells only at dusk when the girls and boys cease to make the garden "trite with their trodding down of its growth" (123); for Lucy views their presence in the garden as a violation of her sanctuary. St. Jean Baptiste sounds a warning in the garden when Lucy, alone at twilight, discovered the love letter, which she momentarily imagines to be addressed to herself.

It is also night when Lucy notices the bell as she dreams of John during the long vacation period. Alone on the street at twilight, Lucy again hears the bell while searching for the home to which Madame Beck has directed her. Somehow, the guilt-ridden city of daylight confusion and dissipation is subdued by the moon's light-bringing radiance and the bell's harmony-restoring sound.

Always, however, a temporary calm or stasis is followed by another crisis. In addition to the structural opposition represented between church and city that reflects a psychological tension within Lucy, *Villette* portrays a structural contrariety among churches also. Although St. Paul's Cathedral and Villette's churches together function as central structures in the novel, they present an interesting contrast in architectural signification.

Why is it that Lucy is able to enter confidently into the dome of St. Paul's, while she faints before "the mass of frontage and giant spire" (192) of the shrine of the Magi? Considering that Lucy finally chooses the moon as her goddess, building for it a church in the sky beyond the transitory city, it may be that St. Paul's is inspiring to her for its resemblance to what the moon later symbolizes for her. Like it, St. Paul's dome lifts her out of the city without removing her from the womb-like, spatial limitations she cannot relinquish for fear of losing her very self, just as she has early in life lost her entire family and means of livelihood.

In the same way that Lucy imagines the crescent moon cradling the globe in its curve, so does she idealize St. Paul's dome as a symbolic delimiter of sacred space, an image consonant with the plan that gave birth to the original city. St. Jean's, however, is as symbolically threatening as are the rats in the attic. A massive frontage and spire suggest the overwhelming oppressiveness of masculinity "flinging its passion against the sky,"[21] whereas St. Paul's dome suggests feminine predictability as does the moon. In its semi-circularity, the dome also functions symbolically as a replica of heaven, since early man envisioned heaven as a dome and built his churches accordingly.

A marriage of soaring spire and sheltering dome, masculine and feminine, is finally never achieved, however, just as St. Paul's and St. Jean Baptiste represent irreconcilable denominational differences across country boundaries. Lucy establishes no final union with either John or M. Paul, a failure that is reflected in her inability to find a home in either city or church.

The former, which threatens diffusion, is countered by the latter which forebodes suppression. Always Lucy teeters on the psychological tightrope between the call of the church to self-effacement on the one hand, and the city's call to self-assertion on the other. Caught in a clash of extreme and opposing forces between fire and ice, city and convent, Lucy subconsciously clings to relics of her past which will safeguard her, she hopes, against the risks involved in giving herself totally to either. Subconsciously she knows she needs the city's freedom to taste life in its fullness, but she also fears losing control. Consequently, she hold herself in ferocious check.

As objective correlatives of this struggle, the church promises protection, while the city threatens alienation. To put it in other words, the center, too restrictive, is countered by the periphery, which is too permissive. Just as injunction with its threat of confinement marks the convent as center, permission with its sense of freedom characterizes the city in its erratic windings. Any resolution must involve a compromise. That final resolution, false though it be, is symbolized by Lucy's geographical move to the Faubourg Clotilde located at the city's limits within hearing distance of church bells and yet within sight of the countryside as well.

Notes

1. Charlotte Brontë, *Villette* (New York: Bigelow, Brown and Co., Inc., 1899), p.52. All subsequent references to this edition will appear parenthetically within the text.

2. Winifred Gerin, *Charlotte Brontë: The Evolution of Genius* (London: Oxford University Press, 1967). According to Gerin's biography, Charlotte admired John Martin's paintings "representing vast perspectives of the lost cities of the ancient world -- Babylon, Nineveh, the Cities of the Plain, Pompeii, seen at the apocalyptic hour of their destruction" because they "satisfied and corresponded to a craving for the grandiose in Branwell and Charlotte Brontë." See Gerin, 434-36

3. H.J. Dyos and M. Wolff, ed., *Victorian Cities* (London: Routledge and Kegan Paul, 1973), xxvii

4. John Keats, "Verse Letter to J.H. Reynolds, 25 March 1818," in *Letters of John Keats*, ed. Robert Gittings (London: Oxford University Press, 1970), pp.80-82

5. U.C. Knoepflmacher, "The Novel Between City and Country," In *Victorian Cities*, ed. H.J. Dyos and M. Wolff (London: Routledge and Kegan Paul, 1973), II, 518

6. In considering the London episode as central, I am in disagreement with those critics who regard that episode as extraneous to the essential plot. One such critic is a Brontë contemporary, G.H. Lewes. See Miriam Allott, ed., *The Brontës: The Critical Heritage* (London: Routledge and Kegan Paul, 1974), p.211

7. Werner Hofmann, *The Earthly Paradise* (New York: George Braziller, 1961), p. 320, 351

8. Gaston Bachelard, *The Psychoanalysis of Fire*, trans. C.M. Ross (Boston: Beacon Press, 1964), p.16

9. Charlotte Brontë, "Gilbert," quoted from Poems by Currer, Ellis, and Acton Bell in *Charlotte Brontë: the Evolution of Genius* by Gerin, p.283

10. The whole discussion about moon and church bells that follows, has less to do with them as emblems of meaning and order for Lucy, than as what Nina Auerbach calls the "equivalent of her desires,

these desires . . . always struggling to break out of control and create their own objects." Lucy, in Auerbach's words, is always "reaching towards a reality that can coalesce into nothing beyond projection." See "Charlotte Brontë: The Two Countries," *University of Toronto Quarterly*, 42 (Summer 1973), pp. 338-342

11. Robert Graves, *The Greek Myths*, Vol.I (Edinburgh: R. and H. Clark Ltd., 1955), p.85

12. Graves, I p.297

13. Alban Butler, *Lives of the Saints,* Vol.VI (New York: P.J. Kenedy and Sons, 1937), pp. 32-34. Also in John Ruskin's *The Bible of Amiens*, the name itself is interpreted as meaning "Glorious Battle-maid," p.56, John W. Lovell, Co. Edition.

14. Yi-Fu Tuan, *Topophilia: A Study of Environmental Perception, Attitudes, and Values* (Englewood Cliffs, New Jersey: Prentice-Hall, Inc., 1974), p.227

15. According to Brontë's biographers and critics, Charlotte wanted Paul dead at the end of the novel. At her father's request for a happy ending, however, she consented to compromise in an ambiguous conclusion to the novel.

16. Nine Auerbach, "Charlotte Brontë: The Two Countries," *University of Toronto Quarterly*, 42 (Summer 1973) p.336

17. Charles Burkhart, "The Nuns of Villette," *The Victorian Newsletter*, 44 (Fall 1973), p.10

18. Charlotte Brontë, "Gilbert," Gerin, p.283

19. Robert Heilman, "Charlotte Brontë and the Moon," *Nineteenth Century Fiction*, 14 (March 1960), p.297

20. Heilman, p.296

21. Henry Adams, *Monte Saint-Michel and Chartres* (Garden City, New York: Doubleday and Co., 1959, p.39

3. *Edwin Drood:* A Boneyard Awaiting Resurrection

Like Villette, where the convent located at the center of the city represents repression as opposed to self-expression, authority as opposed to independence, where passion is metaphorically buried alive in the ghostly nun legend, Cloisterham is also organized about its religious house, in this case a cathedral. In *Villette*, Charlotte Brontë ultimately presents the church, despite its shortcomings, as a guardian of innocence and source of authority in the midst of a city growing without direction or control. In *The Mystery of Edwin Drood*, on the other hand, Dickens presents the church as a dying institution whose life, if it is to know rejuvenation, must now be resurrected in terms meaningful to a growing, changing membership. Dickens' main concern is human psychology rather than institutional reform. Still, the church's presence is significant in relation to those who dwell in its shadow.

Architecturally a monastic structure in which dwellings and church adjoin to form an enclosure against the outside world, Cloisterham Cathedral represents a place of suppressed aggression, buried guilt, and death. Cloisterham, as its name implies, is a secluded place bypassed by history. As a monastic enclosure culturally supposed to preserve what society considered sacred from profanation by city noise and traffic, it is now a mere shell in which the memory of its past lurks within the very stones whose material signs of age reflect a waning of life in the inhabitants as well. Like the Old Cathedral of Bleston in *Passing Time*, a cathedral founded on the ruins of a temple of war, Cloisterham Cathedral also rests on the ruins of military conquest. Beginning with the Druids, and followed by the Romans, Saxons, and finally the Normans, each successive people has added a part to the building before being itself supplanted by a succeeding culture. A heritage of bones is now the Cathedral's only evidence of its former life.

Whereas Charlotte Brontë provides in the city a temporary escape for Lucy Snowe from the repressions of convent living (since city and church represent distinct value systems), Dickens presents city and church as institutions destructive of the person, each infiltrating the other. Lucy finds temporary release from the convent's constraints upon her by rushing headlong into the city. John Jasper, the protagonist of *Edwin Drood*, finds relief in neither, the city of Cloisterham being largely an extension of the church; for the name Cloisterham is the name of the city as well as its Cathedral (a case which is true in Hardy's Christminster as well). In this novel of Dickens, church and city are closely bound up with each other, individuals striving to achieve their identity in spite of rather than with the aid of these institutions. Involuted on itself with limits defined by the church, Cloisterham concentrates in itself the essence of a confusion vaguely sensed in "the city" London, whose diffuseness defies analysis. In *Great Expectations*, for example, London's deceptive attraction is prefigured in Pip's view of the inverted steeple on the distant horizon. The steeple's askew position is explained on the literal level by Pip's seeing it when Magwitch is holding him up by the feet in the country graveyard. Nevertheless, the glimpse foreshadows symbolically Pip's later sensation of the whole city as being awry in its values. In *Bleak House*, too, the demonic in London's streets points to the same at its very soul. Jo, looking up at the "sacred emblem" of the cross on the summit of St. Paul's Cathedral, sees it as "the crowning confusion of the great, confused city."[1] This perception measures the distance of Dickens from Brontë, for where Jo finds only more confusion in looking up at the Cathedral from London's streets, Lucy Snow finds solace in St. Paul's dome as a shelter from confusion. *Villette* provides a vision of the city in which Lucy can be in and yet not of it, a feat she accomplishes somewhat in Villette as well as London.

In contrast, *Edwin Drood* depicts the integral nature of city and church as institutions that have lost touch with the persons for whom they exist. Cloisterham descends from the original city, supposedly a graveyard out of which arose the visible structures of church and citadel symbolic of religious communion with the dead and social communion among the living celebrated there. But while the archetypal city celebrated the life that rose out of death, Cloisterham commemorates the death which follows upon life, for the most part, in its central structures.

The church in its origin grew out of an act of faith (or perhaps terror) in the face of immortality. In either case, its symbols of Judgment and Damnation as well as Life and Resurrection spoke to the individual of a whole society assuming responsibility for a burden and a promise that might otherwise have proven unbearable to each individual alone. Similarly, the city, in its conception as an extension of the church, attempted to transcend the imminent threat of death by making itself as an institution superior to the biological cycles, which confirm man's mortality.

It is against this ideal of transcending mortality that Dickens measures his own century's city and church. In general, Dickens recognizes how pretentious it is for the city to deny its temporal nature when it is the biological and therefore mortal "leaven of busy mother Nature" that keeps "the fermenting world alive."[2] It is, for example, within the City Precincts that those close to the soil naturally celebrate time and death as the necessary preconditions for rejuvenation. In the "vestiges of monastic graves . . .

> the Cloisterham children grow small salad in the dust of abbots and abbesses, and make dirt-pies of nuns and friars, while every ploughman in its outlying fields renders to once puissant Lord Treasurers, Archbishops, bishops, and such-like the attention which the ogre in the story-book desired to render to his unbidden visitor, and grinds their bones to make his bread (22-23).

From earliest times, as fairy tales affirm, mankind recognized death as a source of life. At the heart of Cloisterham, however, there stands a Cathedral which reminds passersby of "Time and Death" (41) without recalling as well nature's promise of "the Resurrection and the Life" (269). With the passing of centuries the promise of life symbolized by lofty stone structures had died in crumbling stone leaving only signs of death and decay. The problem with Cloisterham, city and church, is that it is an institution built for permanence in a world where life is defined by constant change.

The church's failure to instill life within its members and represent life to them as well is manifested by its crypt, where the "'dead breath of the old 'uns'" penetrates nave as well as tower with a damp "earthy flavour" (42). Instead of the breath of life, it fills its members' nostrils with evidence of corruption. In addition to physical decay, a sense of moral deterioration lurks in the shadows and finds a voice in the account Durdles relates to Jasper. According to the story, it was on Christmas Eve, ironically the feast of Life, that Durdles heard a scream of death "followed by the ghost of a howl of a dog—a long dismal howl, such as a dog gives when a person's dead" (125). Later his suspicions of foul play seem verified when he discovers an extra body in Mrs. Sapsea's tomb.

Significantly, a church loses its consecration when murder has been committed within its walls and must be reconsecrated before worship services lawfully may be celebrated there. Having lost its sacred character through defilement, like the Old Cathedral of Bleston discussed in a later chapter, Cloisterham Cathedral receives the attention of "excursion parties" rather than worshipers. And Mr. Tope is as much "Showman" (11) for them as he is verger for priest and worshiper. Suggesting evil, the Cathedral echoes the words intoned by its choir: "WHEN THE WICKED MAN—"(10).

Furthermore, on the morning when Edwin is found ominously missing, the Cathedral is likewise found defiled, the hands of its clock "torn off," pieces of roofing "blown into the Close," and stones from the tower "displaced" (165). Just as the cry of murder was heard on the previous Christmas Eve, it is again Christmas when signs of death and destruction replace expectancies of life. The Cathedral has failed in serving the purpose for which it exists.

Murder, defilement, and a prevailing sense of ruin indicative of the Cathedral's need for a dawn of restoration and resurrection pervade the Cathedral's crypt which seems to await the pick of Durdles' axe as though he were an angel of mercy come to release its bones from bondage. Durdles, who boasts knowing more about the dead than any man living, and is therefore qualified to speak for them, imagines the response of one dead 'un to his knocking on a tombstone: "'I've been waiting for you a devil of a time'" (41). It is indeed a "devil" of a time in Cloisterham for its citizens and members when death and ruin have obliterated all signs of life.

There is not much to separate "dust with the breath of life in it from dust out of which the breath of life has passed" (133) in Cloisterham. It becomes evident that the power of death and the consequences of denying time and change have also penetrated city dwellings, architecturally associated with the Cathedral as they are, and reflecting, as they do, the tenor of the city's sanctuary.

City dwellings reflect the character of those who live within them. A brief overview of the characters, therefore, is necessary before moving on to more detailed analyses of their dwellings.

The overt plot of *Edwin Drood* concerns the question of murder, its detection, and punishment. But a more intriguing way of reading is to follow the clues of the narrator-detective who observes in the city's architecture visible signs of that city's attempts to avoid, deny, transcend, or control time's potentially destructive power.

The first group of characters deals with time and change in a destructive manner. John Jasper, protagonist and choirmaster, tries to escape the necropolis of Cloisterham by plunging into a dimension of existence out of time by entrancing himself in opium dreams, and by controlling others through mesmeric powers. Sapsea, for his part, pretends to have subjected time to his will as city auctioneer and mayor, an office long in his family and as fixed as the pediment over his ancient door. The Nuns' House, in turn, has closed its eyes on time as though blindness can make time itself vanish. Durdles, the city undertaker, capitalizes on time's victims as his means of livelihood, chiseling his home and life out of tombstones. And Deputy owes his identity to serving Durdles.

Only Chrisparkle, Cloisterham's minor canon whose house matches in durability the sound character of its owner, has the vision to see time as the nourisher of life as well as its destroyer. In his house Chrisparkle preserves from destruction time's choicest blessings by storing them for later resurrection. His closet is an index to a mind that choose carefully from among time's fruits and preserves only what has potential for later resurrection and application.

Most resigned to Cloisterham's present condition as a necropolis without need of rebirth is Durdles whose home defines his personality. Resembling the Cathedral crypt, it is like Old Time itself in whose service he is employed as Cathedral caretaker. Unable or unwilling to escape from the outdated institution which gives the city its name, Durdles lives in spirit among the dead. Designer of tombstones and undertaker for the city, Durdles is more of a proprietor than any city landlord and more of an ecclesiastical minister than the "Showman" Tope. Proud that he governs a necropolis, Durdles embodies the crypt itself, dining on tombstones as he does and being "wholly of [its] colour from head to foot." Moreover, his "little antiquated hole of a house," never finished, resembles the approach to "a petrified grave of tombstones."

Making the most of what might otherwise be a depressing business, Durdles likes to pass the churchyard cemetery with a swelling air of ownership. He likes to encourage in his breast "a sort of benignant-landlord feeling" much as Sapsea, the city's mayor, likes to play at being the Dean or the Archbishop of York or Canterbury. To citizens like Durdles and Sapsea, church titles are no more than means of climbing in social prestige rather than offices conferring spiritual responsibility and the mandate to serve. Mimicking the Cathedral itself, Durdles' dwelling is guarded by two sentries who dip in and out of their sentry-box like "mechanical figures emblematical of Time and Death" (41). A pretense of power is Durdles' way of coping with the stark reality of inevitable death. He treats death as a business proposition, and therefore evades its larger consequences.

Durdles is assisted by Deputy, who dramatizes in distorted form an ancient life-renewing ritual as his way of protesting against forces beyond his control. He answers humanity's need for religious ritual by resorting to a primordial practice. That is, he takes relish in stoning "tall headstones": first, because they impress him as being somehow sacred; and secondly, because in his eyes they resemble the living enough to be "hurt when hit" (267).

Beneath this gangster-like prank there lies buried a need once expressed ritualistically by pagan societies. Stone-throwing at a scapegoat symbolically laden with the sins of the people and driven into the desert indicated a purging of the participants. It was believed to be a sacred act which effected what it symbolized. Because Deputy imagines tombstones to be sacred, living beings, his stoning of them gives the kind of relief experienced by primitive people when releasing their feelings of guilt onto a similar object through a similar kind of activity.

Subconsciously, Durdles expresses a need for purgation and deliverance from death by enacting an ancient religious ritual. This action also shows an affinity between modern Cloisterham and the Druidical pagan who practiced human sacrifice. Unable to escape the pervading influence of the Cathedral on his life, Durdles joins its dead ones and Deputy serves Durdles even as he inwardly protests.

In contrast to them is John Jasper, a guilt-ridden citizen of Cloisterham whose respectability forbids his imitating the behavior of Deputy (even though Jasper exercises physical violence against Deputy one night when Jasper is caught off guard). Like the rest of the city dwellings, whose houses are built out of church stone, Jasper's house adjoins the Cathedral by way of Tope's place.

Living midway between Cathedral and gatehouse, Tope is verger for both, since it is his trade to "make the most of everything appertaining to the Cathedral." And Jasper does appertain to the Cathedral much as he resents that association (13). John Jasper's gatehouse, though at a first remove, is composed of the same stone and also lies within the shadow of Cloisterham's Cathedral. In spite of physical proximity, however, "the massive grey square tower" that dominates the scene from any perspective on the horizon is confused in Jasper's mind with an obtruding vision of a "spike of rusty iron . . . for the impaling of a horde of Turkish robbers, one by one" (7). In Jasper's opium-twisted mind, the Cathedral has non-Christian associations buried deep, and indicating some past memory of which he needs purging.

Whatever the memory, it is clear that Jasper's heart is not in his work as Christian choirmaster. Outwardly a respectable member of Cloisterham's religious establishment as its precentor, inwardly Jasper inhabits a world of opium-induced trances, sinister visions, and evil ambitions. Like the dual aspect of the Cathedral itself, beneath whose "grave and beautiful" (64) exterior lie the skeletons of its dead, Jasper has a buried self opposed to the "face and figure" he shows the world, a face that looks "good," but which is dead; for the living Jasper lies in the self concealed from the city (14).

Just as the Cathedral has its literal bones buried beneath the nave where they are hidden from public view, Jasper has a figurative skeleton concealed in the closet of his mind. In a candid conversation with Edwin, he insinuates as much: "'There is said to be a hidden skeleton in every house, but you thought there was none in mine, Dear Ned'" (18).

Living in the shadow of the Cathedral, Jasper lives a secret life in the dimension of his subconscious, which allows him release of those aggressive and erotic drives not acceptable in the daylight world of social convention. At the same time, he has mesmeric powers by which to control others. Instead of feeling the social communion and divine sanction traditionally associated with physical proximity to the church and social affiliation with it, Jasper confesses the deadening effect church affiliation has on his life, a life that is a "cramped monotony" and the sacred music he conducts rather than instilling peace to his soul is "quite devilish." Moreover, he admits to having demons in his heart, which resemble those carved by monks of a bygone era into stall, seat, and desk" (19).

Just as the Cathedral is enveloped in shadow, Jasper's living quarters also lie "mostly in shadow" (14). His principal furnishings—which include a grand piano, music books and bookshelves, and a portrait of Rosa—are seldom touched by the sun. And the wind that ripples the "pendant masses of ivy and creeper covering the building's front" is the same wind that hums "through tomb and tower, broken niche and defaced statue in the pile close at hand" (12). As his house indicates, Jasper lives psychologically in the shadow world of the subconscious as an escape from what he calls "the monotonous round of daylight consciousness and the meaningless routine of church service."

The duality of Jasper's personality, publicly respectable but privately demonic, is reflected in the gatehouse he inhabits. Guarding the entrance between city Close and Precinct, Jasper's gatehouse commands a vision of both periphery and center. Built over the archway, his house has two windows opposite each other. Consequently, when Jasper stands between them, he commands a dual perspective. Like the gateway to his house that opens onto the private and public domains simultaneously, Jasper inhabits the domain of his subconscious even as he leads a life of public respectability. Publicly, he is acknowledged for excellence in teaching and conducting the music whose resonating chords fill the Cathedral. Privately, he is not subject to either law or convention. Like Durdles, who joins the world of the dead past by identifying with the Cathedral, Jasper escapes to a world within where he can live an exterior life of conformity, but an interior one of forbidden pleasure.

Consequently, though Edwin publicly courts Rosa, it is Jasper who possesses her through him. Jasper's ownership of Edwin's portrait of her, and his influence over her as a piano instructor, signify the power he exercises over them both, even though Edwin remains oblivious to it. It is Rosa who shudders at the sound of a chord of Jasper's music and faints at one of his glances.

Then, too, the look of watchful benevolence with which Jasper gazes at the sleeping Edwin is coupled with its hungry aspect. In his relationship with Edwin, Jasper is both benevolent (confiding in Edwin as a brother) and jealous (rivaling with him for the same woman). Because his situation outwardly resembles that of Neville, Jasper confesses to Neville the nature of the jealousy that possesses him:

> You and I have no prospect of stirring work and interest, or of change and excitement, or of domestic ease and love. You and I have no prospect . . . but the tedious unchanging round of this dull place (76).

At this point Jasper does not perceive Neville as another rival for Rosa's hand. And as long as Edwin is alive, Jasper must possess Rosa through his nephew. It is only after Edwin's disappearance that Jasper approaches Rosa directly himself. The mesmeric power of his gaze is illustrated particularly in the convent garden scene. When Rosa looks at him, she feels she is "being compelled by him" (212). There is a look "so wicked and menacing as he stands leaning against the sun-dial—setting, as it were, his black mark upon the very face of day—that her flight is arrested by horror as she looks at him" (214). What makes Jasper so horrible in Rosa's eyes is her recognition of the demon that possesses him; a demon that cannot be exorcised until Jasper is freed from the dualism of his personality, a dualism fostered by outdated institutionalism and conventions that force him to suppress his own psychological needs and drives.

In his opium trances Jasper's demonic drives, publicly concealed, are given full expression. Much as Deputy finds psychic release for his frustrated will to power in stone-throwing, Jasper gets temporary relief in opium-puffing. Falling into a momentary relapse in the presence of Edwin, Jasper makes a rare confession that elicits sympathy from Edwin, but not understanding. For to Edwin, Jasper confesses both a likeness and a difference between himself and monks of old. Both he and they were possessed by demons, but for them the church provided an outlet, whereas for him it provides none. They could take relief in "carving demons out of the stalls and seats and desks," but he would have to look to himself and carve them out of his heart (19).

For Jasper the daylight world of consciousness is too confining and monotonous. He lives, therefore, in the shadow world of the subconscious, a world in which time is abolished; for in his subconscious the same deed can be committed mentally many times and always as though it were the first time; neither does duration limit the amount of experience that can be lived.

Recalling some act of violence committed mentally many times, Jasper expresses surprise when the deed is actually done. He discusses the experience with the Princess Puffer:

> 'Well; I have told you I did it here hundreds of thousands of times. What do I say? I did it so often, and through such vast expanses of time, that when it was really done, it seemed not worth the doing, it was done so soon' (259).

In this shadow world of the subconscious Jasper lives and moves and has his being. Tapping into his subconscious, as Durdles taps the walls of the crypt, Jasper has discovered a secret life principle, like a "spark of that mysterious fire which lurks in everything" (136). Jasper's interior flame, passionate and aggressive, has its external manifestation in the fire he keeps "kindled up" (12) in his gatehouse against the Cathedral's chill, and the spark Durdles manages to strike from the wall of the Cathedral tower to light his and Jasper's way.

Like the windows of his gatehouse, Jasper's eyes are a telling feature of his personality, but instead of radiating light, they reflect darkness. Expressive of a sexual lust forbidden by social taboos, those eyes paralyze Rosa with their mesmeric power as they invade her being, making her their slave. These same eyes look on Edwin with "hungry, exacting, watchful, and yet devoted affection" (15).

Although the narrator is to be trusted in suggesting that Jasper loves Edwin, there is also a suggestion of demonic possession by which Jasper extends his own life through him. The expression "wrapped up in" regarding Jasper's interest in Edwin indicates the possessive nature of their relationship. Then, too, Jasper keeps a diary which is "'in fact, a diary of Ned's life too'" (109), as Jasper himself asserts. A "play of eyes" (77) characterizes Jasper's attention as he follows the verbal quarrel between Edwin and Neville.

Although Jasper stands by as an observer, he is ultimately the instigator of the two young men's mutual animosity. Not only does Jasper administer drinks before the quarrel (perhaps drugged as is the one he prepares for Durdles), but also uses Rosa as a point of contention between them. On the one hand, he insinuates the undeserved hopelessness of Neville's cause in loving her. On the other, he talks about the equally undeserved though promising state of Edwin's, who is destined by parental agreement to marry her.

Like the watchtower he inhabits, Jasper has set himself as master of the fate of others while keeping himself safely immured from mastery. Living through others, Jasper escapes direct implication himself. In such a way he attempts to live within the framework of the institutional church without adhering to its laws in his heart. Through Neville, therefore, Jasper can release his envy of Edwin without himself raising a hand against that relative. So, too, with his eyes Jasper can possess Rosa sexually without actually violating her body and therefore exposing himself to public recrimination.

With his eyes that control, possess, and manipulate, Jasper enjoys a view of Cloisterham from its Cathedral tower and fears Cloisterham's stone-thrower, the one assuring his superiority to time and transience, the other threatening subjection to it. From the top of the Cathedral tower, for example, Jasper has a comprehensive view of Cloisterham with "its ruined habitations and sanctuaries of the dead at the tower's base; its moss-softened red-tiled roofs and red-brick houses of the living . . . " (136-37).

Most especially, however, Jasper contemplates "that stillest part" (137) including his own gatehouse; for Jasper is acquainted with the person beneath the respectable exterior he shows to the world. Jasper's nature, which thrives on seeing without being seen, is therefore most threatened when that "baby-devil" (as Jasper himself calls him) Deputy calls out after him: "'I'll blind yer, s'elp me! I'll stone yer eyes out, s'elp me! If I don't have yer eyesight, bellow me!" (140). Losing one's eyes is the classic, upward displacement of castration, both sexual and psychological. Even though he is misled by following his own interior drives, Jasper is not confined to the narrow existence defined by society for a churchman. Such an escape is encouraged by an ecclesiastical institution which is both overly restrictive and unbending with regard to change.

Jasper and Durdles are not the only ones, however, whose houses lie in the shadow of the Cathedral. The whole city is built out of church stone: "Fragments of old wall, saint's chapel, chapter-house, convent, and monastery, have got incongruously or obstructively built into many of its houses and gardens, much as kindred jumbled notions have become incorporated into many of its citizens' minds" (23).

Sapsea, too, participates in these ruins of time. Though he is unaware, his establishment mirrors his outlook. Somehow he is convinced that the pediment above his door has the power to deliver him from death, since it has withstood the onslaughts of time undiminished. He loves "the chastity of the idea" (35), the permanence and stability of the pose which represents himself as surely as it does his father before him.

Unchanging, one generation asserts the immortal character of the other. So, too, the weather-glass prepares him in advance against the invasion of any foreign element of nature. Finally, Sapsea foolishly enthrones his clock as though it can give him control over time itself. For him, the city over which he reigns as mayor is an impregnable fortress of which his house is a mirror. His speech, too, echoes his conviction that nothing changes, at least nothing he cannot control by mechanical means. To his way of thinking, what was appropriate in his infancy is "appropriate to any subsequent era" (36). Consequently, Sapsea is comfortable with the institutional church whereas Jasper needs a dual personality to cope with it.

Opposite Sapsea's establishment on High Street and opposed to it in vision is the Nuns' House, which counters Sapsea's "self-sufficiency and conceit" (34) with naivete. The most prominent feature of this establishment is the brass plate on its gate which reminds "imaginative strangers of a battered old beau with a large modern eyeglass stuck in his blind eye" (24). Old, worn, and blind, the image of an apparently unsuccessful suitor on a convent gate speaks of the Nuns' House as a participant in the church's denial of time; for the effects of time are visible on the convent gate as they are in the cathedral's interior described as "the throat of Old Time" (74).

By refusing to grant entry or even to see the forces of change working beyond its doors, the Nuns' House may pretend to transcend time, but even the ignorance of a granite pillar cannot deny the effects of time on all things created. Thus, for example, in the Nuns' House as in the convent on the Rue Fossette, infractions of the rule requiring virginity (that vow symbolic of time transcended) have caused fractures in the structure. The ghostly nun who appears to Lucy when she is tempted by sexual fantasizing, and who paid for her own violation of the vow by being buried alive, enjoys a thematic resurrection in *Edwin Drood*. The narrator, for instance, muses about the possibility of nuns being "walled up alive in odd angles and jutting gables of the building for having some ineradicable leaven of busy mother Nature in them which has kept the fermenting world alive ever since" (24).

Fear of participation in such a fermenting cycle is evident in Miss Twinkleton's secret dalliance with a certain Mr. Porter, a dalliance supposedly concealed by the darkness of night, since Miss Twinkleton prizes her image as impeccable directress of the former convent. Rosa's fear of Jasper is largely of a sexual nature as well. Even though Rosa preserves her bodily integrity, she feels the diabolic power of Jasper's glance, a glance that compromises her innocence by its penetrating potency.

Although he remains an unsuccessful suitor, Jasper is not blind, but frightfully perceptive in exercising power over her. At the same time, her broken engagement to Edwin, surrounded by more immediate causes as it is, represents ultimately Rosa's fear of experiencing her own sexuality, of undergoing the maturing process that will separate her from the Nuns' House, that hothouse for roses in their budding stage.

Denial of sexuality in this church-affiliated House is denial of life itself. Rosa, raised within these walls, is also victim of its fears and denials. She will consent to kiss Edwin only after they have agreed to love each other as brother and sister rather than as husband and wife. And when Edwin arrives to see Rosa, Miss Twinkleton "turns to the sacrifice" (26) to announce his arrival. Aware that from the convent's point of view her virginity is in imminent danger of being lost, a deplorable state to be moaned if not avoided, Rosa covers her head with her apron in bashful reticence when entering Edwin's presence.

When Rosa does seriously contemplate the prospect of marriage to Edwin, her mind immediately suggests images of death, since their home, as she envisions it, will be Egypt with its "tiresome old burying grounds" (32). The blind eye on the Nuns' House gate constitutes a reticence on the part of the ladies within to surrender their guarded innocence for entrance into the biological cycle implied by entrance into adulthood.

Whether in marriage or permanent virginity, however, old mother Nature continues the fermenting process. A refusal to participate cannot prevent time from working changes that are fast making the Nuns' House as obsolete in function as it already is in name.

The evidence of fermenting mother Nature can also be found in Crisparkle's home, but with a difference. His home, Minor Canon Corner, also lies in the shadow of the Cathedral's general influence. But the Cathedral rooks that fly overhead, and the sound of the bell and organ penetrate his walls with a mellowing effect on its owner. He is the model Dickens sets up as a healthy response to an institution in a state of demise.

Unlike the spark of fire that lurks within the recesses of the Cathedral, the kind of flame characteristic of Jasper's nature, Crisparkle's personality has about it the quality of the lamplighter's dot of flame. Even though sepulchral gloom dominates the Cathedral, the city's lamplighter still makes his silent, nightly round. Cloisterham "would have stood aghast at the idea of abolishing" this ancient tradition, even though its citizens regard "the sacred shadow" cast by his ladder when caught in the fire's glow as an "inconvenience" (130).

Although his house forms part of the Close and his dwelling is "not a stone's throw" (74) from Jasper's, Crisparkle has managed to integrate his personality within the daylight world of consciousness. As an outlet for his repressed, inner needs, Crisparkle engages in a program of physical fitness, which includes boxing, swimming, and jogging. Into the gloom of the ancient city's general state of decline, Crisparkle brings the sunshine of charity and creative endeavor.

His house, like his person, is a picture of stability rendered harmonious by time's mingled consonance and dissonance. Although Crisparkle is a minor character as far as the novel got written, Dickens may have intended him as a norm against which to appraise the other personalities of Cloisterham. On the outside Minor Canon Corner mirrors the Christian athlete who dwells within. Its brick walls covered with "strong-rooted ivy" enclose small rooms rendered mighty by "big oaken beams" (53). Within its "strong-walled gardens," the same trees that yielded fruit for monks of a bygone era continue to bear fruit for Mr. Crisparkle and his mother.

The strength of his house outside is matched by its integrity within. Although Jasper teases Edwin with the insinuation of "a hidden skeleton" being locked up in the closet of every house, Crisparkle's closet is as accessible to inspection as his home is open to guests. His closet, where he keeps his health-sustaining preserves, has "a crowning air . . . of having been for ages hummed through by the Cathedral-bell and organ until those venerable bees had made sublimated honey of everything in store"(101). Crisparkle has extracted and preserved the best of the ancient Cathedral's produce. His closet is like a city in miniature in which every jar and bottle is a "benevolent inhabitant" whose integrity is revealed by wearing "his name inscribed upon his stomach" (100).

Association with Crisparkle likewise brings out one's best qualities; for when one comes forth from his shelves, he comes out "seeming to have undergone a saccharine transfiguration" (101). Honeythunder, the professional philanthropist, reveals in his name the contradiction that is rectified by Crisparkle, the true though unprofessional philanthropist who supports Neville when society prematurely condemns him. Living within time's narrowing confines, Crisparkle is a connoisseur of its hidden potential, preserving the sweetness it yields and doing what he can to distill good even from the bitter that comes with the sweet.

Crisparkle's house, like himself, embodies Cloisterham's potential for a rejuvenated faith in the Christian values of honesty and integrity. Although Minor Canon Corner occupies only a corner with a house on it that contains just a closet for all his preserved treasures, it is like a stained glass window in the Cathedral with its property of diffusing light on a sunny day. Sometimes in summer there is such a day when "the Cathedral and the monastery ruin show as if their strong walls were transparent, when "a soft glow seems to shine from within them, rather than upon them from without"(221).

More often, however, the Cathedral calls attention to its general interior rather than to its illuminated stained glass windows. The general impression when entering the Cathedral then is like "looking down the throat of Old Time" (94). As a focal statement describing what the Cathedral is in contrast to what it might be, the passage warrants being quoted in full:

> Old Time heaved a mouldy sigh from tomb and arch and vault; and gloomy shadows began to deepen in corners; and damps began to rise from green patches of stone; and jewels, cast upon the pavement of the nave from stained glass by the declining sun, began to perish. Within the grill-gate of the chancel, up the steps surmounted loomingly by the fast-darkening organ, white robes could be dimly seen, and one feeble voice, rising and falling in the cracked monotonous mutter, could at intervals be faintly heard (94).

Significantly, when the Cathedral's jewels of light cast upon the pavement are fast-fading with the declining sunlight, the windows of homesteads shine with the "brilliance of beaten gold" (94). In the same say, Crisparkle's home is like a jewel of light reflected from the Cathedral.

When the institutional church no longer provides an adequate guiding light to its members, it is to the individual that Dickens turns. Crisparkle serves as a model of Christian deportment and uprightness. The city as a whole remains in need of purgation. It is in the disappearance of Edwin Drood that the city's guilt is revealed and, in the exposure of that guilt, readied for its expurgation. Because of Edwin's mysterious departure from Cloisterham and the violent nature of Neville's previous animosity toward him, suspicions of foul play and cries of "'Bloodshed! Abel! Cain!'" (188) resound through Cloisterham's streets.

Subsequently, like the Biblical Cain, Neville is banished from society to go "withersoever he would, or could, with a blight upon his name and fame" (185). The curse placed on Neville is, in truth, a displacement of the curse of Cain that lies over the whole city of Cloisterham, much like the curse under which Bleston lies in *Passing Time*, a novel parallel with Edwin Drood in its detective motif as well as in the Biblical Cain motif.

Rather than admit its own complicity in a crime whose social nature demands expiation by society as a whole, Cloisterham's citizens find a scapegoat. Neville, an outsider with a history of violent behavior, becomes the likely choice. Yet in spite of the city's success in driving Neville out, guilt remains. For society's mental stoning of Neville is a bogus one, whereas Deputy's is a justified defiance of a society blameworthy in denying him all social and religious communion. And until the true murderer is found (if there is one, since Edwin may have escaped with his life[3]) the whole city bears the mark of Cain.

Although they may not be directly responsible for Edwin's disappearance, Rosa, Grewgious, and even Crisparkle unwittingly precipitate it. By their secrecy concerning the change in wedding plans, Rosa and Grewgious make possible a murder motivated by jealousy. For the thought of Edwin actually marrying Rosa and taking her off to Egypt may be just the outrage Jasper can't bear. Even Crisparkle, Cloisterham's model of true charity, shares responsibility in that he introduced Edwin and Neville, an acquaintance which ends in Neville's threat to kill Edwin. Such a threat is just the alibi Jasper needs to commit the murder himself and turn the accusing finger against Neville. If guilt is to be purged, someone beyond suspicion and personal prejudice in the matter must be called in from outside. In the meantime, until the guilty one is removed, the whole city remains under suspicion of guilt, under the curse of Cain.

The curse promises to be removed, however, by a "private eye," who soon moves into the city to purge it of its guilt and to restore innocence. Although Dickens never lived to complete the novel, my conjecture is that Tartar is probably the detective Datchery.[4] Tartar's suitability for the job is manifold.

A former lieutenant at sea, that great symbol of time's relentless flux, Tartar has proved himself superior to the sea's destructive forces. Even after his transfer back to a landed existence, Tartar remains relatively untainted by the city in his rooftop paradise. An outsider with clear, unbiased vision, Tartar fulfills the requirements of a good detective. As a "private eye" who must be above the situation he is sent to investigate, Tartar is again suited for the job.

Like the word 'detect' which means literally "to remove roofs," Tartar is equipped to perform the job of detecting as his dwelling above the city's roofs indicates. A past history at sea and a present existence in the sky over London equip Tartar for the job of detecting and removing the curse of death from the city of Cain.

Water, whose destructive power has taken the life of Rosa's mother, washed up the only remains of Edwin's body, and threatened the life of Crisparkle, is turned to good use by Tartar, who uses water as a condition of rebirth. Although others succumb to its devastating properties, Tartar derives life from it, as his daring rescue of Crisparkle and successful career at sea testify.

Above the city is Tartar's little corvette of a home, a beanstalk paradise, and a ship that stays afloat above the city's flood. Over the streets that are "so strange and crowded," so "gritty" (221), Tartar has built a private "man-of-war" (236) in which everything is shipshape. There are no "blushes among the fruits of the country of the magic bean-stalk" (237) Tartar has grown. Neither is Rosa quite sure "how she ascended (with his help) to this garden in the air, and seemed to get into a marvellous country that came into sudden bloom like the country on the summit of the magic bean-stalk" (235).

Moreover, Rosa believes "that his far-seeing blue eyes looked as if they had been used to watch danger afar off, and to watch it without flinching" (234-35). In his eyes alone Tartar will be a match equal to Jasper. In contrast to Jasper's spellbinding, penetrating gaze that paralyzes Rosa in a fear that is largely of a sexual nature, Tartar's gaze dispels the possibility of even a blush on Rosa's face, for his eyes are not controlling. Instead of being possessive, Tartar's eyes have the power to ward off danger even at a distance. The Ogre of Cloisterham that continues "to grind their [men's] bones to make his bread" (23) seems about to meet his match in this Jack who goes by the name of Tartar.

Even a city as black as London (that "great black city" which "cast its shadow on the waters" (247) like the bridge of death spanning life) is made at least momentarily green by the magic of Tartar's ingenuity and kindness. In contrast to the river in Cloisterham, which Jasper watches from the tower as it is "winding down from the mist on the horizon with a restless knowledge of its approach towards the sea" (137), the river down which Tartar rows Rosa and Grewgious seems to lead them to "some everlasting green garden" (247). Instead of denying temporality, Tartar redeems it, knowing, as he does, how to rise above circumstances both figuratively and literally.

The order he builds above London's streets "so gritty and so shabby" (222) is indicative of his ability, like Crisparkle's, to discover and preserve the spirit of life, which is not subject to corrosion or decay. Here the curiosities he has rescued from various sea voyages are each "displayed in its especial place, and each could have been displayed in no better place" (236). With his ability to transcend life's death-dealing forces and create order with a vision that is both keen and perceptive, Tartar seems a likely candidate to double as Datchery the detective.

Although Cloisterham Cathedral emphasizes death in its architectural ruins, empty nave, and crypt full of bones, there is the hope of a resurrection, a rebirth that must come through individuals, however, rather than through a social or religious movement. For just as detection and removal of the murderer in the city is equivalent to opening city closets and having their skeletons revealed, grave-opening (a necessary clue to the solution of Edwin's disappearance) will symbolically reestablish the church as a potentially life-affirming institution through its openness to change and renewal.

Even though Dickens satirizes a character like Sapsea, who denies temporality and death in his boasting and in the external show of his dwelling, Dickens does not deny the possibility of transcending mortality. Surprise over death's occurrence "even in the city"[5] as Mr. Dombey explains to his son, emphasizes a secular refusal to see the dead as citizens, an attitude foreign to the ancient city founded on the graveyard as a means of symbolic communion between the citizens of both worlds. In *Edwin Drood*, Durdles' "Tombatism" (42) is an ailment to be cured rather than a natural condition to be accepted in this city with its roots in antiquity. As Datchery begins his job of lifting Cloisterham out of its curse of darkness and guilt, "a brilliant morning shines on the old city. Its antiquities and ruins are surpassingly beautiful, with a lusty ivy" (269) gracing its walls in contrast to Jasper's shivering climbers lost in shadow. Civilization and nature unite in expressing the renewal of life.

Without the passage of time, the seed that is sown in death cannot come to flower and fruition. Something besides ruin and decay does remain as a result of time's passing, a faith to which Crisparkle's closet bears witness. Including every delicacy from jams and spices to pickles and wines, his closet of preserves combines "all its harmonies in one delicious fugue" (100). And that which makes him nauseous is kept separately and accepted for its medicinal uses.

In a rapid transition from the mundane to the profound, the narrator compares Crisparkle's willing submission to this "herbaceous penitentiary" with that of "the highly popular lamb who has so long and unresistingly been led to the slaughter." Like the Lamb of sacrifice (in Christian symbolism, the Lamb of God) in whose blood believers are ritualistically purified, Crisparkle would go from that closet to Cloisterham Weir and ascend again as hopeful of being cleansed "as Lady Macbeth was hopeless . . . of all the seas that roll" (101).

Reminiscent of Tartar's rooftop garden and the "everlastingly green garden" (246) to which he rows Grewgious and Rosa, Cloisterham itself seems to breathe the air "from the one great garden of the whole cultivated island in its yielding time" about the time that Datchery arrives. Like the city, the Cathedral's earthy odor is subdued as it then preaches "the Resurrection and the Life." Even "the cold stone tombs of centuries grow warm, and the flecks of brightness dart into the sternest corners of the building, fluttering there like wings" (269).

Participating in the dynamics of the labyrinth, the bewildering city of London, which gives Rosa the impression of always "waiting for something that never came" (252) is peripheral to Cloisterham, the secluded center where life's essential mystery, that of life rising out of death, is explored and reaffirmed.

Although Dickens never got so far, it is safe to deduce from the available evidence that the demons will be expelled by the work of Datchery, whose chalkmarks are already showing his progress in arriving at the truth concerning Edwin's disappearance. According to the notebooks Dickens left behind, and the testimony of his biographer and close friend John Forster, Jasper was to confess.[6] Through his delivery, Cloisterham may also be delivered from the same demonic possession and experience a rebirth.

Notes

1. Charles Dickens, *Bleak House* (New York: New American Library, 1964), p.283

2. Dickens, *The Mystery of Edwin Drood* (New York: New American Library, 1961) p.24. All subsequent references to this edition will be noted parenthetically within the text.

3. Charles Sugnet, "Private Virtue and Public Guilt in the British Novel," Diss. University of Virginia, 1970. A well-known critic who also took the stance that Drood would reappear was Anthony Proctor in *Watched by the Dead: A Loving Study of Dickens's Half-Told Tale*. Critics who agree that Drood was murdered, but propose varying solutions for the identity of Datchery, include the following: W. Robertson Nicoll, *The Problem of Edwin Drood: A Study in the Methods of Dickens* (London: Hodder and Stoughton); J. Cuming Walters, *The Complete Mystery of Edwin Drood: The History, Continuations, and Solutions* (London: Chapman and Hall, 1912). This last-named book contains at its conclusion a table providing a list of all major critics writing from Dickens' death until 1912 concerning each one's position regarding Datchery's identity, the fate of Drood, and other enigmatical data related to Edwin Drood.

4. Critics in agreement with my supposition that Tartar is Datchery include Percy Carden and G.F. Gadd. Both represent early 20th century views. See Percy Carden, *The Murder of Edwin Drood*, intro. B.W. Matz (London: Cecil Palmer, 1920). G. F. Gadd, "Datchery, the Enigma: The Case for Tartar," *Dickensian* 2 (Jan. 1906) pp.13-16. Also Gadd, "The History of a Mystery: A Review of the Solutions to `Edwin Drood,'" *Dickensian* 1 (Sept, Oct., Nov., Dec. 1905) pp.240-244, 270-274, 293-297, 320-323. Plate of Jasper's Gatehouse 3 (March 1906) p.64. After the first third of the century, however, critics generally dismiss Tartar on the basis of his being an outsider and therefore unfamiliar with Cloisterham's topography and citizenry. It is precisely their argument against Tartar's being Datchery because he is an outsider that forms the basis for my argument in his favor. My stance is influenced by W.H. Auden's summary of the characteristics

common to all detectives in great detective fiction. See W.H. Auden, "The Guilty Vicarage," *Harper's Magazine* 196 (May 1948) pp.406-412

5. Dickens, *Dombey and Son* (Harmondsworth, England: Penguin, 1970), p.153

6. John Forster, *The Life of Charles Dickens*, Vol.III (London: Chapman and Hall, 1972-74)

4. *Jude the Obscure:* An Unattainable Dream

Jude the Obscure explores the Biblical image of the City of God's chosen bride. Jude envisions his union with Sue Bridehead, "the city's phantom," as a type of the union between heaven and earth, the City of God joined to the City of Man.[1] For Jude, distance makes both city and woman eminently desirable. Detained on the periphery of the great city, Jude eagerly anticipates a future that will fulfill his apocalyptic expectation. It is possession of the city, like possession of a woman in marriage, however, that will yield disillusion.

The motif of city and woman as seductive, promising fulfillment at a distance and then eluding his grasp when claimed, has its adjunct in the mythic labyrinth whose obscure windings Christminster mimics. Fittingly, it was an act of seduction which caused the building of the mythic labyrinth in Crete. Pasiphae, desiring to unite with divinity disguised in the form of a bull from the sea, seduced him by entering the body of a wooden cow. As punishment for this act of seduction, this act of taking advantage by deception, Pasiphae and her monster-child were imprisoned in this labyrinth. Christminster, like the labyrinth, is a city of deception for Jude the dreamer, who perceives only its sacred character.

Coupling the Biblical concept of city as bride with the mythic notion of labyrinth as bridewell, Hardy places Christminster at the center of Jude's dream of paradise, which ends in tragic entrapment. Moreover, the thematic interplay between Hebraic and Hellenic world views contained within Christminster involves Jude in a tension that proves irreconcilable. Reverencing the classical purity of Greek culture but immersed in Hebraic convention, Sue Bridehead incorporates in her name and character the split between the Hellenic and Hebraic, the lily and the bride. Acquaintance with Sue personifies Jude's experience of Christminster, both, in turn, testing the quality of his soul.

In brief, *Jude the Obscure* recounts the seductions of a dreamer who exposes himself to labyrinthine byways believing they must lead to and enclose a harmonious center made sacred by culture and dreaming. In its very name, Christminster implies its sacred character as a "church of Christ." Jude anticipates his journey to this holy city as though Christminster were a treasure to be acquired at a great distance. As in all his novels, Hardy follows the double thread of "distance and desire — distance as the source of desire and desire as the energy behind attempts to turn distance into closeness."[2] In these terms Jude dreams of the "long circular perspective ending in the shining disk of quivering water at a distance of a hundred feet down." Proportionately high as his goal is inaccessible, Jude's hope takes him away from his village green located "nearly in the centre of the little village" (27), to a more distant and therefore more enticing center.

Just before this brief reverie, in which he perceives himself gaining social prestige and intellectual recognition by joining the ranks of Christminster's College of Scholars, Jude had watched enviously as Phillotson, the local schoolmaster, left Marygreen for Christminster, the reputed center of learning. Only after Jude sacrifices all he owns for this same city, does he, like Phillotson, discover its seductive nature. Even then, however, he cannot separate himself from this mistress of his dreaming. The city which at a distance lures him with the prospect of "beautiful music everywhere" becomes, as he approaches more closely, the center of his own life where all around him "there seemed to be something glaring, garish, rattling." Here where he expects harmony, Jude finds a place where "the noises and glares hit upon the little cell called your life, and shook it, and warped it" (39, 33). Phillotson's disappointment, prefigured in the piano, the source of musical harmony he is forced to leave behind, will be Jude's as well. In fact, Jude and Phillotson function as doubles in several ways. Besides the dream of intellectual enlightenment in Christminster they both cherish, Jude and Phillotson also desire the same woman, herself the living spirit of contemporary skepticism inhabiting the tradition-conscious Christminster.³

Jude clings to his idealistic dream, direct experience to the contrary notwithstanding. Observing the birds in the field, for example, Jude comes to the conclusion early in life that in nature one creature's fortune is another's misfortune. Looking to the city as a way out of such inscrutability, Jude dismisses "nature's logic [as] too horrid for him to care for" (33). Shortly thereafter, his ability to dismiss nature's way in favor of the city's is tested in his encounter with the quack doctor Vilbert.

Breaking faith, Vilbert fails to produce the books promised in return for Jude's services. Intent on his one goal, however, Jude fails to recognize that Vilbert's duplicity has some relation to Christminster, which he claims proudly as one of his centers. The possibility that nature's capricious logic might rule city as well as country life does not enter his mind. Minor as this kind of trickery may seem it is an early instance of the kind of major seduction to which Jude later yields. In fact, not even after his life is ruined does Jude concede that the city's law is as inscrutable as nature's. It is Phillotson, his double, who confesses: "'Cruelty is the law pervading all nature and society; and we can't get out of it if we would'" (299).

After recovering from the disappointment of Vilbert's trickery, however, Jude succumbs to a more serious temptation in the sexual wiles of Arabella, a modern version of the mythic Circe, who turned men into swine, as well as the Biblical Delilah whose seduction transformed a dauntless giant into an impotent weakling. Sitting in a tavern with Arabella, Jude notices "the circular beer-stains on the table," an ironic reminder to the reader of the pure, "quivering water" shining at the bottom of the well, a vision from which Jude is already being led astray (57).

Even as he is being seduced, however, Jude believes himself moving closer to that wellspring of pure harmony, the well's circular perspective of vertical striving tempered by its horizontal call to rest. In truth, however, Arabella's natural attraction begins to obscure this vision so that he temporarily forgets Christminster. Lying on the summit of a hill with her, Jude could have seen "the distant landscape around Christminster," but he "did not think of that then" (63). Jude's actual yielding sexually to her begins in a walk "to the circular British earth-bank adjoining," ground consecrated by the bones of the dead, but is consummated in the house of the pig farmer where Arabella and Jude no longer hear "the chime of church bells" calling worshipers to church services elsewhere (65). Following the desires of the flesh, Jude is temporarily deaf to the call of the sacred and spiritual that wells from his interior depths.

Even Jude's suicide attempt following the disastrous outcome of Arabella's seduction and their subsequent marriage, a union later considered as a "fundamental error" (77), is an act based on deception. Having found "a large round pond," Jude tests the ice for safety; discovering that it "cracked under his weight," certainly therefore too thin to support him, Jude "ploughed his way inward to the centre" and jumped (78). Contrary to all expectation, however, the ice itself seduces him by refusing to receive the bulk of his weight beneath its fragile surface; the center holds.

Although Jude fails to recognize the significance of this irony, the narrator perceives that for good or evil, life is subject to forces beyond man's control. Jude, however, believes in the existence of a city where he will be in control of his own fate, and therefore refuses submission to Arabella, "nature's logic" in the flesh.

After leaving this country wife, Jude enters the city where he undergoes the more subtle enticements of Sue, whose power over him is nonetheless real for being spiritual in nature. Although Jude perceives her charm as angelic and therefore salutary, it is actually she who undermines his allegiance to traditional Christian values and turns his face toward those of pagan antiquity. In an episode that carries symbolic weight, Sue comes to his lodging late one night and exchanges her wet clothes for his dry ones after which she sleeps on his bed until morning. Even though she is forbidden fruit against which he has been warned by his Aunt Drusilla, Jude finds himself magnetized by her spirit, which he subconsciously shares. In her, Jude becomes conscious "of having at last found anchorage for his thoughts," even though her philosophy is a pagan one; for, on occasion, Jude finds himself addressing pagan divinities through her influence (98).

Attracted to each other as "two parts of a single whole" in their mutual understanding, each externalizes the suppressed desires of the other (276). Often when Jude is thinking in terms of a Christian philosophy, Sue extols a pagan life style. When, on the other hand, Jude begins to recognize the beauty of classical antiquity, Sue confesses her allegiance to a Christian philosophy.

The statues which Sue smuggles into her lodging in Christminster personify her pagan philosophy; she would be Venus, goddess of love and beauty, and he her Apollo, god of light and music. Like Jude's ideal city visualized in his mind as a cultural and religious center where learning will provide answers to mend the breaches between God and man, Delphi, Apollo's city located at the center of the world, is the mythic place where answers, equivocal as they might be, are given.

The site of a new city, for instance, was selected by the Greeks through consultation with the Delphic oracle. The image of the city as both Biblical bride and mythic center of the world is projected onto Christminster, Jude's star in the East within whose center he will find the answers to nature's projected onto Christminster, Jude's star in the East within whose center he will find the answers to nature's puzzling questions. Jude dreams of acquiring the light of understanding within the walls of the city's university and then sharing that light with others as religious minister. Sue, however, is already closely associated with the city of Christminster by name and occupation at the time of Jude's arrival, even though her spirituality is not Christian.

In his pursuit of Sue, Christminster's phantom, Jude discovers the city's divided nature—its pagan heart overlaid with Christian architecture. For she enters "with her heathen load into the most Christian city in the country" (100). Publicly, however, she is identified with the city's ecclesiastical warehouse as an engraver. At the same time, Sue considers Christminster's university as a church of learning in ruin, its buildings having "an extinct air . . . accentuated by the rottenness of the stones" (87).

This duality within Sue reflects a duality within the city itself and ultimately an irreconcilable division within Jude between his profession of Christian ideals and the basically natural values by which he lives. Consequently, Jude's Aunt Drusilla plays a Cassandra-like role in warning Jude first to forget his dream of going to Christminster and secondly, to shun acquaintance with his city cousin there. As though by instinct, Drusilla urges Jude to accept the obscurity of country living with its predictable biological rhythms as opposed to the city's capricious uncertainty.

Although Sue, the pagan temptress, exerts a powerful influence over him, Jude knows that his Christian heritage makes it "glaringly inconsistent for him to pursue the idea of becoming the soldier and servant of a Christian religion" (208) as long as he and Sue are as close as "one person split in two" (220). But whereas Sue openly admits that her philosophy of life is innately pagan and only conventionally Christian, Jude, in fact, secretly shares her skeptical attitude toward Christianity. Ultimately, however, both believe in the dream of finding an earthly city that will reconcile the laws of nature and man, the inner needs with the outer reality.

Contrary to Jude's reverence for Christminster's walls which embody a long tradition of Judeo-Christian theology, Sue's room with its Greek statuary signifies her longing for a return to nature and classical antiquity; Sue longs "to get back to the life of [her] infancy and its freedom" (140). Unable to bridge the gap that separates them as pagan from Christian, mistress from wife, Sue and Jude reflect Christminster as a city divided against itself. Accumulated symbols from a venerated past no longer answer present needs, if they ever did.

When she explains her way of thinking to Jude, Sue speaks of Christminster's intellect as "new wine in old bottles," the "old bottles" being its medieval heritage which she believes "must go, be sloughed off," or the whole city itself "will have to go" (149). In the end, however, when pressed by circumstances and convention, Sue renames her statues of Venus and Apollo as Magdalen and Peter. In spirit she remains essentially pagan in her thinking, but to all appearances she returns to the tradition of the Christian fold by rejoining Phillotson. In the guise of a repentant Magdalene and a Peter upon whom no church will be built, the two finally separate.

Aware that his path to the city has been obstructed by women, Jude wonders if it is their fault or that of society:

> 'Is it, he said, 'that the women are to blame; or is it the artificial system of things, under which the normal sex-impulses are turned into devilish domestic gins and springs to noose and hold back those who want to progress?' (209)

If women entrap Jude by obeying the laws of nature, their allurements are less seductive then those of the city which he conceives as having transcended nature's capriciousness. Even before seeing Christminster, Jude has mentally clothed her in splendor befitting a bride. Talking to a workman tiling a roof along the road to Christminster, the young Jude inquires of the city he cannot see through the mist even from the top of a ladder: "'The times I've noticed it,'" responds the tiler, "'is when the sun is going down in a blaze of flame, and it looks like— I don't what.'" Jude's imagination having already raced ahead, he finishes the comparison: "'The heavenly Jerusalem,'" he suggests (55).

Later when the workers have left, Jude prays for and receives a glimpse of this city jeweled like John's Apocalyptic vision:

> The air increased in transparency with the lapse of minutes, till topaz points showed themselves to be the vanes, windows, wet roof slates, and other shining spots upon the spires, domes, freestone-work, and varied outlines that were faintly revealed (36).

In his dream, "as gigantic as his surroundings were small," Jude continues to behold "the new Jerusalem, though there was perhaps more of the painter's imagination and less of the diamond merchant's in his dreams thereof than in those of the Apocalyptic writer" (36). In such a city Jude imagines even the rain being different, not dreary as in other cities. And the smoke rising in the sky will have about it "the mysticism of incense" (37). Whereas Lucy Snowe, in *Villette*, fears the church in the city as a "Babylonish furnace" that will harm, Jude embraces *the image of the city* with its church steeples as a

"Nebuchadnezzar's furnace" (37), a place where fire ignores the laws of nature and therefore does not consume, a fire that transforms a furnace into a holy place of singing men.

Likewise, the voice of the city calls to Jude in the sound of its bells as it also called to Lucy Snowe. Although they rang out a warning to her, however, Jude interprets their message simply as "'We are happy here!'" (37). The ominous sound of city rain and church bells which threaten to invade Lucy's privacy or to impose limits on her personality, fails to dampen Jude's spirit or disturb his composure until rain eventually causes his physical death and the bells that ostensibly ring in the city's festivity ironically announce his death to that same inattentive city.

Before his final despair, however, Jude's dream, stronger than reality, continues to draw him on as the star in the East enticed the wise men of old. In fact, Jude does encounter three men who seemed to be coming from the direction of Christminster. As Jude "pointed to the light in the sky—hardly perceptible to their older eyes," they accommodate his wish to believe whatever he wishes: "'Yes. There do seem a spot brighter, in the nor'-east than elsewhere, though I shouldn't ha' noticed it myself, and no doubt it med be Christminster,'" one replies in the name of the trio (38).

While Jude remains on the circumference longing to get in, the city itself appears as a halo, a circular band of light emanating from a sacred center which he can only glimpse from a distance. Within the holy aura of the city, however, Jude envisions a state of harmony, "beautiful music everywhere" and freedom from the hindrances and ridicule of a rustic countryside.

Finding the obscurity of country living unendurable, Jude seeks the enlightened way of the city: "As the halo had been to his eyes when gazing at it a quarter of an hour earlier, so was the spot mentally to him as he pursued his dark way" back to the hamlet. This Heavenly Jerusalem, his dream deferred but not dismissed, is "a city of light"; and an Eden before the fall where "the tree of knowledge grows" (39).

Having dreamed a city comparable in magnificence to the apocalyptic vision of the heavenly Jerusalem, Jude, like the animals he pities, is destined to fall into the gin, the seduction of his "mistress," Christminster, the dust of Jerusalem's walls (38). Consequently, when darkness envelops her at their first face-to-face meeting, Jude glories in her "gray-stoned and dun-roofed" (86) appearance, a validation of his earlier reading of her as an "ecclesiastical romance stone" (47).

Even though her only sparkle is that cast by a "vane here and there" visible in the sunset rather than the church steeples seen from afar, Jude venerates her profile "of sober secondary and tertiary hues" (86). Catching sight of the city lamps "which had sent into the sky the gleam and glory" he dreamed of in former days, Jude notices now how their "yellow eyes" wink at him "dubiously," as though having begun to tire of waiting for him so long.

In fact, he wonders if "they did not much want him now"; but that wink is a fleeting one (86). Like Revel in *Passing Time*, who is lost in the city without a map, and Lucy in *Villette*, who also loses her way in the darkness of London and Villette, Jude reaches for the map with which he is equipped, only to find it is too dark to read it. The difference between Butor's vision of life and that of his nineteenth century predecessors is that whereas Brontë, Dickens, and Hardy perceive some pattern to be followed or grid in which to fit, Butor undermines the presupposition that there is one.

Consequently, although Jude cannot "see enough to decide on the direction he should take to reach the heart of the place" (87), daylight will show the way. Unable to find the center at night, Jude is condemned only temporarily to labyrinthine wandering with its "many turnings" and "dark corners" as the city "encircled" him. Even though darkness overtakes him, Jude refuses to acknowledge his blinded condition; for when "he passed objects out of harmony with [the city's] general expression, he allowed his eyes to slip over them as if he did not see them." As Jude "serpentined among shadows," he wandered into "obscure alleys, apparently never trodden on by foot of man," being fragments of entry ways which seemed to him incapable of housing modern thought in their "decrepit and superseded chambers" (87).

Though his first glimpse of Christminster is a bleak one, Jude's glorious vision of a city of light remains intact.

Discouraging as first impressions are for Lucy and Revel, Jude finds himself in sympathy with the city's fallen state and even encouraged by its need for restoration. It is only with daylight that he recognizes its likeness to a cemetery. While some of its buildings resemble "family vaults above ground," others are "wounded, broken, sloughing off their outer shape in the deadly struggle against years, weather, and man" (91).

Rather than submit to the jarring conflict, "the glaring, garish" opposition between the outer reality and his inner dream, Jude sets about making that dream a reality by rebuilding the city's walls (33). For him it is "encouraging to think that in a place of crumbling stones there must be plenty for one of his trade to do in the business of renovation" (91). As he begins the task of rebuilding these walls that house his dream, Jude continues to believe that within them lies the "unique centre of thought and religion—the intellectual and spiritual granary of this country" (116). Borrowing the phraseology of theologians and doctors of the church in defining the godhead since the twelfth century, Jude speaks of his dream city as the "silence and absence of going on [that] is the stillness of infinite motion—the sleep of the spinning top" (116).

To others both within and without the center, however, Christminster is perceived quite differently. To an outsider it is nothing but "auld crumbling buildings, half church, half alms house, and not much going on at that"(116). To another it is a Tower of Babel, a confusion of facts such that its citizens can no longer understand one another: "'O they never look at anything that folks like we can understand,' a carter informs Jude, "' On'y foreign tongues used in the days of the Tower of Babel, when no two families spoke alike'" (38).

Christminster's uninitiated consider their taverns "the great palpitating centres of Christminster." Church structures crumble around them, but the taverns are being "entirely renovated and refitted in modern style." Here Jude meets Tinker Taylor, a "bankrupt ecclesiastical ironmonger" (174), who has found a home in the tavern, since he and the church no longer have any use for each other.

For Sue, on the other hand, the center of the city's life is the railroad station. When Jude asks her to sit in the Cathedral with him, she answers that she'd "rather sit in the railway station" since that is "the centre of town life now" (136), the Cathedral having had its day.

Unfortunately for Jude, the historical process, irreversible as it is, has taken its toll on the city as it crumbles from the center outward, as it too participates in the biological cycle of birth, growth, and death, despite man's vision of the city as eternal.[4] As the earthly city began, so will it end: Ashes to ashes, dust to dust. What may have been good centuries ago is now played out, much as Sue would like to keep alive a spirit of antiquity. Although Jude believes he is fortifying the walls of a living city as a stone mason, he is in reality restoring cemeteries; for he lives and works among the dead rather than the living, of whose presence he remains oblivious:

> Although people moved round him he virtually saw none. Not as yet having mingled with the active life of the place it was largely non-existent to him. But the saints and prophets in the window-tracery, the paintings in the galleries, the statues, the busts, the gargoyles, the corbel-heads—these seemed to breathe his atmosphere (93).

Shut out from the life of the living, Jude can hear the echo of his own footsteps "smart as the blows of a mallet" on the pavement outside (93). Although forbidden entry into the world of scholarly learning, Jude knows "more about those buildings materially, artistically, and historically, than any of their inmates: and consequently feels himself unjustly condemned to merely restoring their crumbling surfaces (93). What never occurs to Jude is the possibility that maybe there is no more than shell. Unwittingly, he may be patching a carcass that contains no soul. Christminster is perhaps no different from Marygreen, Melchester, Shaston, Alfredson, Aldbrickham, Stoke-Barehills, or any other city he has visited or may visit.

The local church in Marygreen, for example, has finished the cycle which the church in Christminster is destined to follow. In the hamlet of Jude's birth, "the original church, hump-back, wood-turreted, and quaintly hipped," has been reduced to "heaps of road metal in the lane, or utilized as Pig-sty walls, garden seats, guardstones to fences, and rockeries in the flower-beds of the neighborhood" (27), a condition obtaining in the city of *Edwin Drood* as well. But Jude, his mind darkened there by brighter visions elsewhere, does not read the message before him in Marygreen's ecclesiastical architecture. A "hump-backed church whose contours coincided with those of nature has been replaced by an urban structure which has obliterated the past, projects no future for itself, and serves no purpose in the present.

A modern builder from London, an "obliterator of historic records," has reduced "the ancient temple of the Christian divinities" to a "green and level grass-plot" and its surrounding graveyard to "eighteenpenny cast-iron crosses warranted to last five years" (28). The new church of stone built to replace the old serves merely as a sounding board to echo the surrounding noises, like the clacking of the paddle on Jude's hind parts for allowing God's creatures to feed in the farmer's field.

This church, sponsored by the monied, like the farmer who exploits Jude, stands as a modern-day testimony of "love for God and man" (31). Only after Jude has completed his circuit of cities on the circumference of his map around Christminster and returns to Marygreen does he finally recognize that the burial ground itself has lost its ancient character as a sacred plot of ground. His Aunt Drusilla is "put into the new ground, quite away from her ancestors," while the undertaker bustles through the "simple ceremony . . . having a more important funeral an hour later three miles off" (202). In one of his final visits, Jude is greeted by a "churchless churchyard, now abandoned," in which the ivy leaves overgrowing the wall peck at each other. From his room Jude can see "the vane on the new, Victorian-Gothic church in the new spot" which has "already begun to creak" (127).

Like a moth circling a flame, however, Jude's spirit belongs to Christminster. Hovering on various points of the circumference, Jude anticipates alighting at the heart of the fire that burns without consuming like Nebuchadnezzar's furnace or the burning bush before which Moses removed his sandals, since he was walking on holy ground.

One of these points on the circumference is Melchester, an ecclesiastical city founded as a Roman military outpost, which serves as a temporary retreat for Jude after Christminster's initial rejection of him. Like Marygreen, however, Melchester is a cemetery experience; for his first work there is "some carving at the cemetery on the hill," which is followed by "the Cathedral repairs, which were very extensive . . . "(137).

When Jude, having arranged to see Sue there, proposes that they go for a walk, she rejects Melchester's prospective: "Not ruins, Jude— I don't care for them" (137). Although Melchester's condition actually reflects the "wasting walls" of Christminster, Jude is blind to the fact (30).

Another city on one of the many points of the circumference surrounding Jude's dream city is Shaston, itself "the city of a dream" (193), as the narrator quotes Drayton concerning its ancient foundations. As with Marygreen and Melchester, however, its chief attraction lies in its dead past, in its ruins and the graveyard which is itself associated with a church in its geometric perspective.[5] To the eye of the beholder its ground "slopes up as steeply as a roof," rising above the church in front of it. Such is the illusion it creates that the inhabitants of Shaston jest about their cemetery lying "nearer to heaven than the church steeple" itself (194). Embodying on a smaller scale Jude's experience of Christminster, tavern and cemetery have replaced the church as the city's intellectual and spiritual center.

An old legend of the city insinuates the ironic truth that lies behind the city's ostensible excuse for vacating its church on Sunday. According to the story, the tavern's centrality followed inevitably when "the inhabitants were too poor to pay their priests, and hence were compelled to pull down their churches, and refrain altogether from the public worship of God; a necessity which they bemoaned over their cups in the settles of their inns on Sunday afternoons" (194). Symbolically as well as geographically closer to Christminster than Marygreen, Shaston is a city without wells, a significant fact in light of the dream-inspiring well that occupies a central location in Marygreen.

In contrast to the pure water of Marygreen's well, Shaston's well is dry. Consequently, it has to import its water supply at a price, beer flowing more freely than water in Shaston. Living in this city where spiritual values lie buried as deeply as its pure water supply and monastic foundations, Sue feels "crushed into the earth by the weight of so many previous lives there spent" (196). This city, which was once the home of pagan temples and famous Christian abbeys visited by numerous pilgrims, now serves merely as a temporary resting place for "wandering vans, shows, shooting-galleries, and other itinerant concerns, whose business lay largely at fairs and markets" (194). Undaunted by all this modern restlessness and fanfare, however, Jude sets out to restore here, as elsewhere, the medieval ruins of the city's church.

It is Sue, not Jude, who recognizes that moulds don't necessarily fit shapes, that for people as well as buildings civilization's moulds often have no relation to the shapes that must fit them. Nevertheless, just as Jude is unable to break the mould of his dreaming, as he sets about restoring the masonry of old structures, Sue, wedded to Phillotson, is helpless to escape the cultural accretions that "ponderously overhang a young wife who passed her time here" (199). Sue regrets that modern man can no longer live by nature's rudimentary laws of "gravitation and germination" (140). She likes to envision herself as an Ishmaelite, a wanderer on the face of the earth. But, in reality, she is "an urban miss," one who has been formed within the closures of civilization (140).

Not unlike the Biblical Ishmael who was thrown into an empty well, Sue finds herself confined by the walls of an outdated tradition. Jude idealizes these walls as shells containing the pearls of medieval and modern scholarship, the wisdom of great thinkers. Sue, on the other hand, discounts such pearls as insignificant in light of antiquity's purity. When, for instance, Jude clings to the idea of living in Christminster because its scholarly men "loom so large" in history there, Sue responds: "'Yes,—they do. Though how large do they loom in the history of the world? . . . What a funny reason for caring to stay'" (108). Unable to find the "quivering water" (27) of "infancy and its freedom" (140) within Christianity, Sue looks to the ancient past before the corrupting influences of history took hold of church and city. Jude, however, remains "Joseph the dreamer of dreams as Sue calls him (198).

Whether Marygreen, Melchester, or Shaston, Jude continues to hover on the periphery, believing that the shortcomings of the smaller cities will be redeemed by the splendor of his holy of holies among cities, Christminster.

Another significant point on the circumference which ironically mirrors the center itself is Stoke-Barehills. Located at the center of an imaginary triangle whose points represent a county seat, an ancient capital, and a military outpost, Stoke-Barehills epitomizes the state of the city as a necropolis, for, according to the narrator, its "most familiar object . . . nowadays is its cemetery, standing among some picturesque medieval ruins beside the railway." A highway from London once passed through the city but is no longer in use. Not unlike Christminster, its "modern chapels, modern tombs, and modern shrubs [have] a look of intrusiveness amid the crumbling and ivy-covered decay of the ancient walls" (273).

Christminster itself is a carcass for dead bones as indicated by the names of its buildings. Jude takes note of "Mildew Lane," "Sarcophagus College," and "Rubric College." The walls of these buildings, "silent, black, and windowless," cast "four centuries of gloom, bigotry, and decay into the little room Jude has acquired for Sue (313). For him, however, the city continues to sweeten the air with the remembrance of its great Christian scholars, such as "Newman, Pusey, Ward [and] Keble" (108).

To his gaze, the lichened, "time-eaten" walls of the colleges are like prose transformed by age into poetry. Consequently, there is hope for him in mere waiting: "How easy to the smallest building; how impossible to most men," he concludes (92). Suffering from "the modern vice of unrest," however, Jude is determined to stop at nothing less than penetration within those walls where he supposes scholarly study will fulfill his dream (92). Although Jude believes he is progressing from point to point on a circumference that spirals toward the center, the narrator perceives the labyrinth in which he is trapped.

Alfredston, for example, prefigures "the Fourways" of Christminster where Jude can survey a geographical vista of Christian colleges in one direction, a mental vision of ancient palaces in another, Arabella in a third direction, and Sue in a fourth. Appropriately, Jude meditates as he approaches such places in the road:

> At Fourways men had stood and talked of Napoleon, the loss of America, the execution of King Charles, the burning of Martyrs, the Crusades, the Norman Conquest, possibly of the arrival of Caesar. Here the two sexes had met for loving, hating, coupling, parting; had waited, had suffered for each other; cursed each other in jealousy, blessed each other in forgiveness (121).

In each setting Jude looks to the past as a way of decoding the meaning of the present. But whether that past is embraced from its endpoint in present ruins or at its source in ancient conquest, there is little light for the future when one grasps a general view of men, seeing "their whole rounded lives rather than their immediate figures" (262).

Father Time, the personification of history, is a murderer of truth, for he wears "the tragic mask of Melpomene" (265), who, as one of the nine muses, had the gift of speaking false things that seemed true. Seductive in its pretense of progress, time has the cumulative effect of multiplying "Thou Shalt Nots" as is illustrated in the anecdote of the church painters who, by omitting all the "nots" in the Ten Commandments, affirmed Time's record of sin, thereby creating such a scandal that the whole building had to be reconsecrated to appease the congregation (285). On "Remembrance Day" in Christminster, Jude is made aware not of rejoicing and achievement, but of "Judgment" and "Humiliation" (306) as he looks back on his own dream short-circuited by the "freezing negative that those scholared walls had echoed to his desire" (314).

Though still determined to see his vision fulfilled, Jude acts like the Biblical St. Stephen, "who, while they were stoning him, could see Heaven opened" (198). Although Christminster, "the City of learning," wears "an estranged look," Jude convinces himself that he has "never seen the place look more beautiful" (173). Like the bride he will never possess in Sue Bridehead, Jude loves the city the more as it eludes his embrace.

Sue, is, in fact, a figure of the city, its phantom when he is deprived of its physical presence. Besides calling him Joseph the dreamer and St. Stephen, Sue compares Jude to Don Quixote, another dreamer who pursues his ideal in spite of ridicule, rejection, and isolation. Like Quixote, who was sorry the world was not as he thought it should have been, Jude, too, has set out to restore what he considers a defaced image.

More than all these, however, Jude resembles his namesake Judas Iscariot, who dreamed of Christ as the promised Messiah who would build the kingdom of heaven on earth. Jude proposes to help in accomplishing this mission, not by following the way of the lowly carpenter of Nazareth, but by imitating the victorious Messiah in his triumphal entry into Jerusalem. There Jude himself will sit among the doctors, listening to them, and asking them questions. And all of them will be astounded at his wisdom.

Unlike the poor Christ who lived most of his life in obscurity, Jude will fulfill the expectation of the Messiah's disappointed disciples. Redeeming the failure of the historical Christ, Jude addresses himself in the Biblical words once spoken to Christ from the clouds of heaven: "'I'll be her [Christminster's] beloved son, in whom she shall be well pleased,'" he promises (50). He too plans to begin his ministry at the age of thirty, "an age which much attracted him as being that of his exemplar when he first began to teach in Galilee" (132). Like a triumphant Christ, Jude will "come up to Jerusalem to see the festival" (310). In short, Jude will write his own version of the New Testament; for he says to Sue: "'Will you let me make you a new New Testament, like the one I made for myself at Christminster?'" (151)

Though it is valid in some respects, the parallel between Jude and Judas, both intent upon a heavenly kingdom, breaks down in another. Unlike the historic Judas, Jude's spirituality is colored by paganism. As the narrator puts it: "The atmosphere blew as distinctly from Cyprus as from Galilee" (98). When approaching a crossroads, Jude ponders whether to take the ancient Roman or the modern Christian way. And on Alfredston Road, Jude requests to meet his pagan Sue, since her "up-train" and his "down-train" cross literally as well as symbolically at that point (173). Alfredston is itself a crossroads between modern Christminster and ancient Marygreen.

The final irony of the city's rejecting Jude is his inability to recognize that repudiation as final. When its academic doors close him out, for example, he turns to manual labor as a restorer of its crumbling walls. That failing, he resorts to his childhood occupation as a baker, but a baker with a dream. Jude's cakes are special because they are shaped like the "windows and towers and pinnacles" of Christminster (294). From building with stone, he turns to supplying the city with bread. Although Father Time recognizes the college buildings of Christminster as jails, Jude sees them as cloisters. Even as he lies on his deathbed in Arabella's house, Jude listens enviously to the faint sound of speeches coming from the city where its doctors are conferring honorary degrees on its chosen sons.

Christminster, with neither "Christ" nor "Minster," is a false dream, but one that Jude nonetheless refuses to relinquish. To live without that dream would be to die, just as he chooses to do when deprived of Sue, who had opened windows where all else was walls, even though she, too, finally betrays him by enclosing herself within the walls of conventions she had formerly defied.

Within faint hearing distance of the city's speeches and festivity, Jude is also within hearing distance of its bells. The first time Jude heard them he was a mere boy living in Marygreen. From that distance he imagined they were calling to him "'We are happy here'" (37). Later when he actually heard them within the city itself, he counted one hundred and one strokes instead of the anticipated one hundred, the last stroke being an inadvertent mistake, he reassured himself then. Having found Christminster's only center in a tavern, however, he eventually learns to count the last stroke of the bell as a coincidence of "gratuitous irony" (178).

Such a reminder of his failure to find the city's center in its church is an unwarranted act of cruelty when the fault lies not with himself but with time and circumstance, both as much beyond his control as his given name, Fawley (folly). Jude's dream of connecting is a dream worthy but impossible of attainment. In terms of Jungian psychology, Jude's plan is to make the dream of the silver disk, the circular perspective, a reality. To circumscribe a crossroads and thereby make its center tangible is simultaneously a way of uniting the vertical and horizontal at their point of intersection. In terms of the historical reality of the city, Sue voices Jude's frustration in failing to achieve this harmony when she says: "'At present intellect in Christminster is pushing one way and religion the other; and so they stand stockstill, like two rams butting each other'" (150).

Christminster, its halo seen in a vision from afar, takes visible shape as a series of broken lines in "crocketed pinnacles and indented battlements" along "obscure alleys" (87). In this supposed center, as on the circumference, disjointure characterizes the relationship between man and the universe in which he lives; what is "good for God's birds [is] bad for God's gardener" (31).

The prospect of entering the sacred enclosure is no more than a dream for Jude. And without such a center of reference, the periphery is no more than "the home of lost causes" (89). Even though the city, together with its church, fails to fill the emptiness of Jude's restless longing for "the sleep of the spinning top," still he continues to renew "the crumbling freestones of mullioned windows he would never look from, as if he had known no wish to do otherwise" (323).

Though Jude's son may be "the beginning of the coming universal wish not to live," he himself continues to address the city's phantoms as though they are really his friends and, in turn, hears their voices respond in the deserted streets (317).

For Jude, and Hardy his creator, the greater curse is not that man dreams, but that the labyrinth of reality is bound to seduce the dreamer by leading him on with expectations of a sacred center never to be attained. A stanza from one of Thomas Hardy's poems entitled "On a Fine Morning," expresses the theme concisely:

Whence comes Solace?—Not from seeing
What is doing, suffering, being
Not from noting life's conditions
Not from heeding time's monitions;
But in cleaving to the Dream,
And in gazing at the gleam
Whereby gray things golden seem.

Notes

1. Thomas Hardy, *Jude the Obscure* (New York: Collier Books, 1962), p.174. Subsequent references to this edition will appear parenthetically within the text.

2. J. Hillis Miller, *Thomas Hardy: Distance and Desire* (Cambridge, Massachusetts: Belknap Press of Harvard University Press, 1970), xii.

3. In *Hardy, A Collection of Critical Essays*, Albert Guerard, ed., A. Alvarez discusses the image of Jude as magnified and lit from different angles in the characters of Phillotson and Sue, who are extensions of himself rather than fully drawn characters in their own right.

4. Robert Dickinson, *West European City: A Geographical Interpretation* (London: Routledge & Kegan Paul, 1951), p.254

5. Dickinson, p.254

5. *Passing Time (L'Emploi Du Temps):* A Life-Sustaining Myth

If Dickens's Christminster is bemoaned as an unattainable dream, Bleston of *Passing Time* is an inferno. A fictional city set in England with architectural dimensions consonant with its geographical landscape, Bleston is ultimately a city of texts to be read and cryptograms to be decoded, a city whose psychological as well as literal atmosphere is heavy with leaden wetness and whose reservoir of mythic art, history, and achieved culture reflects in visible shape humanity's psychic projections, mankind's attempt to transcend mortality.[1] Through its art and architecture Bleston summarizes man's collective experience and the various meanings attached to it by the way one century imposes its philosophy on another in a continual flux of transformations from one generation to another. Just as the whole atmosphere of Bleston symbolizes its present state of spiritual apathy, the city's mythic remnants stored in museum and cathedral attest to the value, but finally to the inadequacy of old myths in interpreting present reality. The correlation and contradiction, linkage, and breakage between past cultural models of signification and present attempts to interpret them is the subject of Revel's diary. In the words of Victor Hugo, "a moment arrives in all human society when the sacred symbol is worn out and obliterated beneath the free thought, man escapes from the priest, and the excrescences of philosophies and systems gnaw the face of religion."[2] Although Butor himself does not seem to subscribe to any system, Revel constantly tries to establish his identity within the Greco-Roman, Judeo-Christian heritage of his adopted city.

What motivates Revel's careful scrutiny of Bleston's deposit of myth is his fear of being swallowed psychologically by the waters of the Slee (Styx and Lethe) and losing his identity in a city which, after six months of breathing its "bitter, acid, sooty" air and drinking its insipid, muddy water, has already begun to engulf him in its own lethargy and monotonous routine.[3] Against the fear of mental paralysis and amnesia, against his fear of being adopted as one of Matthews' Sons (Matthews and Sons having employed him as translator), Revel turns to the city's treasure house of Hellenic and Judeo-Christian myth wherein society has embodied symbolically its entry into the Great Time, a time out of time, mortality, and transience.[4] There one can find, through identification with the culture heroes of myth, lives of cosmic significance and colossal endeavor worthy of emulation. Revel hopes to revitalize himself and the necropolis of Bleston, whose demise he subsequently welcomes as a necessary prerequisite for resurrection, struggling at the same time, however, to preserve himself from the immolation. With the eyes of a religious geographer Revel envisions himself repeatedly as a Theseus who has the thread which then eludes him so that he must cling to another one. The thread which he thinks should lead him to the center (perceived in myth as the source and end of life, and the place where the forces of life conquer death)[5] eludes his grasp. He is not satisfied with meaning that is only partial, temporary, and conditional, as his attempt to write a chronologically accurate diary and a geographically correct map testify.

The first possible center of which Revel becomes aware is Alexandra Place with its trinity of stations enclosed in a circular plaza, geometrically symbolic of wholeness. Because its bridges arching over the streets "looked like so many gates in an enclosure," Revel fancies he "must be in the heart of Bleston" (11), already thinking in labyrinthine terms and placing himself in the center as he does. Trying to find his way to Matthews and Sons on the following day, however, Revel attends as his landlady directs him to the Old Cathedral. But he reminds her that his new place of work is near the center of the city, i.e., Alexandra Place.

On the map which he later purchases, Revel notices that Bleston boasts three centers: Alexandra Place, the Town Hall, Matthews and Sons, and the New Cathedral, and a third known as Old Bleston, containing the Old Cathedral. Whereas currently it is Town Hall Square that is "obviously the hub of the town's activity" (51), he is informed that ten years ago, it was the tenth district that was Bleston's most fashionable center, which now contains Great South Cemetery, itself as large as "an average-sized town" (41). In referring to the Town Hall, Revel continually remarks on its "ridiculously crenelated black towers" (51) that strike him as architecturally incongruous with its present function. Moreover, it is the Town Hall that has replaced the Old Cathedral, if only for a time, as the topographical center of Bleston. Representing the modern industrial city in general, Bleston mirrors a trend in which the town hall becomes the city's outward symbol in modern times "as surely as the medieval church had been in the past."[6]

All this confusion about where the true center is in this Blestonian labyrinth is compounded further when Revel surmises on first appearances that Alexandra Place with its three railway stations forming a geometric triangle must be Bleston's center. In addition to its name, which tantalizingly suggests the labyrinth's historic origin in Egypt, Alexandra Place is designated on Revel's map by an incomplete circle, thus defining the Place as a central enclosure, a conclusion Revel will later have to reverse as a result of further information.

In spite of Revel's curiosity concerning the whole city, he is soon drawn to the Old Cathedral because he thinks he is going to the place that ought to be the center, considering its origin in a medieval world where the cathedral was the civic as well as religious center of urban life. Captivated by The Murderer's Window, which depicts in stained glass the myth of the triumph of Cain, Revel repeats his visits in ritualistic fashion, hoping thereby to gain insight into Bleston's origins and his misery. A product of the sixteenth century, fixed by John Ruskin as the century in which "churches were first built to the glory of man, instead of the glory of God,"[7] The Murderer's Window emphasizes the founding of the city of man by Cain, who is also reputed to be the father of the arts of music, weaving, and metalwork.

Abel's Window, on the other hand, which originally occupied a position of equal importance opposite that of Cain's, is now completely transparent. Abel, whom Augustine associates with the city of God, remains only inadvertently through a record of the social festivity which accompanied the installment of his window, the stained glass being later destroyed by an angry sixteenth century mob. This apparent triumph of the city of man over the city of God dissolves the mythic ties of city to sacred order.

Moreover, Cain's City rose as an act of defiance against the God of the ancient Hebrews, who was conceived as a God of nomads, Abel's God. They were to be a pilgrim people on this earth and citizens of a heavenly city rather than an earthly one. Only after the violation of the covenant established between God and His chosen people was Jerusalem built. Subsequently, the mythic ties of the city to a sacred order were undermined. Abel's blood, therefore, cried out to God for vengeance against Cain, and put a curse on the soil out of which his city grew.

The city of Cain, glorified in the Old Cathedral's window, a window of Renaissance workmanship dedicated to man's glorification of himself rather than God, wears the mark of defiance. The city's sin is the greater, to borrow Ruskin's image, "because . . . done in the face of the House of God, burning with the letters of His Law."[8] The words "Mene, Mene, Tekel, Upharsin" (78), just barely decipherable on one of the windows, is the warning against defiance of that Law. Literally translated as "He is numbered, he is weighed, they are dividing," the modern equivalent is "weighed in the balance and found wanting."[9] Impending doom is inscribed in the glass.

The blood of Abel crying out from the earth for vengeance is also mirrored in the reddened skies of history, whose record of destruction is depicted in the windows that line one side of the cathedral's ambulatory: Athens, Sodom, Gomorrah, Baalbek, Babylon, Timad . . . . . Nor does Bleston escape complicity, that city symbolic of the modern city generically. For just as it served the sixteenth century artist as a model for Cain's City with its reddened sky, its buildings are daily being consumed in flame as Revel walks its streets. Instead of Abel's window balancing this view of the city of man with a view of the city of God, the view through the now clear glass is that of Bleston, a mirror image (with some gaps caused by time) of that same Bleston used as a model for Cain's City. It is the priest who calls Revel's attention to "the outlines of the old gabled houses under the darkening sky: which can be seen through the "clear glass" that once told in stained glass "the stories of Abel and Seth" (75). At the oldest center of Bleston, then, already is to be found the beginnings of disintegration.

In Bleston, dedicated to the glory of man through technology (Cain as mason and Tubalcain as metalworker) and art (Jabal the weaver and Jubal the musician), man is still "Profugus in terra," a wanderer and a fugitive even in his own city. Instead of music, one still hears "the hoarse rattle" (74) of death and destruction, the price of mortality. In the accursed city of Bleston music itself reverses its traditional role. Instead of the Old Cathedral's bells calling the city to worship and driving away demons (as the bells' function was conceived by the medieval mind), their ringing has caused one side of the tower to collapse, thus damaging the ambulatory and destroying the four windows depicting the cities of the damned. Symbolically, God's judgment against those cities is thus erased by the obliteration of the cities themselves. Bells, once conceived as images of order, have become instruments of demonic confusion.

To read the text of Bleston symbolically as I have just done in interpreting the bells' significance, however, is to fall into the very trap *Passing Time* warns the reader against; for to spin such a web out of life's random heterogeneity is to bind oneself within a fabricated pattern. Although we have no other choice than to make some patterns, we should realize their tentative and temporary nature.

Perhaps the case of the bells is an example of a natural law being violated, followed by a technological remedy applied. For when the bells prove too large for the tower, they are replaced by an "electric carillon." The danger is to make too much of an event. Bells, the "very essence of their city," inscribed in the city's coat of arms, and signified in the interpretation of Bleston as "Bells Town," may have no more significance than the simple facts just related (81). Reversals of this kind are characteristic of the game Butor plays with his reader, the contest Revel engages upon with the city, and the labyrinth which is the figurative board on which both games are played. Butor's labyrinths include directional reversals, mirrors, doubles, and stylistic repetitions.

In the cathedral, or anywhere, for that matter, where one's right is always another's left, Revel observes the game of reversals played by time and perspective. When Cain, the reprobate, for example, is on Revel's right, Abel is necessarily on his left. Similarly, on his left are all those windows that once showed "the holy cities," cities traditionally associated with the right side. Like Abel's window, these too have been destroyed. In both cases, the Old Cathedral has become a labyrinth in which the righteous are confused with the sinister. In the case of Abel's window, the bishop, "paralyzed by some doubt, some scruple, some sudden dread" (80) had been left blind and dumb by the destruction he had witnessed. The stoning of Abel's window was a sinister, literally left-handed act, which relegated a righteous one to the fate of the damned.

Moreover, the windows themselves tell a story of inverse significance. Rome, for example, occupies a window on both sides of the ambulatory. The multiple reversals possible confound what might otherwise be a simple dichotomy. In response to Revel's questioning, his guide responds: "'Yes, Rome the Imperial City; opposite it on the other side, on the left of the choir from where we stand, but on the right of Christ the Judge in the big east window, was Rome the Papal City, the capital of the Church'" (78). Appropriately, each window tracery is pieced within "a close, tangled network of leads" (77), a miniature labyrinth. In the windows of the Old Cathedral, then, there is a thematic reversal of the Biblical story that is duplicated by a spatial reversal as well. For, while "Cain's window is in a perfect state of repair," Abel's has been stoned out.

In a similar manner, the cities of the righteous and damned are spatially reversed from Revel's perspective. Most importantly, however, the whole significance is reduced to a matter of position. Although the original intention of the cathedral's artist was to organize the whole from the perspective of Christ seated for the Last Judgment, that window has never been executed. What is this book of Genesis in glass if not an obliteration of the original text as succeeding generations showed "through their illustration of the official Biblical text that they themselves had read something else into it?" (79)

What defines the sacred center for one generation does not necessarily hold for another. Or to use Yeats's expression, "the center does not hold." The Renaissance, for example, did not restore to life a mythic heritage lost during the Middle Ages; for myth had always remained vital. Rather, it is always, then as now, a question of reinterpretation and reintegration of the old myth into the changing culture. Myth survives through reinterpretations that accord with humanity's changing knowledge of the universe.[10]

Although myths may have suffered distortion through the passing of successive generations, they continue to live, at least fragmentarily, as the embodiment of man's search for the center of significance in life's psychological labyrinth of uncertain turnings and blind alleys. In the Old Cathedral the search itself has practically ceased. No work of restoration, completion, or replacement is in progress. Furthermore, it shares the emptiness of the museum, that storehouse where artifacts are preserved in a cultural attempt to preserve its memory by orderly classification. As he enters the Old Cathedral, Revel notes the empty pews, the three giggling girls on tour, and a few scattered vigil lights burning. The scheduled devotion will draw no more than a handful for the priest who will "have to take evening service at five o'clock for a dozen worshipers" (77).

Revel is convinced that the priest he encounters reading his office will be of no help to him in explaining the meaning of the myth he studies in the symbols of the cathedral's windows. As it turns out, the priest alone is initiated, knows his way in the labyrinth, and offers to assist Revel. In Revel's case, the very fact of having to ask the meaning is to be living without it, which is part of his misery in Bleston. Then, too, the cathedral's "little black lobby reeking of dust and always damp," introduces him into the nave through a "creaking door, padded with imitation leather" (205). That "great morass of slimy dust" which is the city, has penetrated into this putative House of God (35).

Displaced from home, Revel falls into the mud on the slippery, liquid-mud steps of Bleston's Old Cathedral. It is this act that marks his entry into and participation in the city's fall, a fall inherited from Cain. He experiences a guilt that leaves him feeling "polluted by the creeping fog" of the city. He fears being "deserted by the man that [he] had once been" (54) before arriving in Bleston.

Murder gives the Old Cathedral its *raison d'etre*, just as murder gives the detective his. Revel's identity in Bleston is sustained by his desire to take vengeance on the city that threatens his own existence with its "rudderless amnesia" (35). Consequently, like the detective who commits the final murder by exposing the murderer, Revel's hands are covered with the blood that spills over Cain's tunic onto the floor of the cathedral:

> The red blood streamed like a slow downpour through the red sky above the city, behind Jabal's looms, behind Jubal's orchestra, behind the forge of Tubalcain; then it spilled out from the Window over the walls and paving stones, even over the pews, even over my hands, most of all over my hands, which were covered and steeped in thick luminous redness, like a murderer's hands, in the center of the pool of blood, my hands in the center of the bloodstain spilled from the scene above, in the silence (205).

Its ancient center founded on the site of a temple of war, a brother killing brother, Bleston remains "Belli Civitas" and continues to swell without limit like the amoeba it is, with its Prison showing like a vacuole on Revel's map of the city, "a sort of negative of the gleaming mark imprinted on Cain's forehead" (272). While Revel looks for and often finds doubles to aid him in matching the thread of his personal meaning with that of his mythic mentor, Bleston itself is perceived only as an aborted mimicry of some meaningful past. In this city Revel feels like "a mere virus lost amidst its filaments," like a scientist "armed with this microscope to study this huge cancerous growth" (41) whose nuclei inevitably partake in the disease of the cells.

Although his study of its stained glass, its "close, tangled network of leads" (77), sheds some light (literal and symbolic) on his understanding of the labyrinth which is Bleston, it provides Revel with only a tenuous clue in his task of gradual unraveling, an unraveling which might just as easily be a reveling in the labyrinth where reversals, mirrors, and photographs confuse reality with its imitation; for to unravel is only to weave something else.

In addition to its desecrated Judeo-Christian center, which is in a state of disrepair and neglect, Bleston has some Roman history buried under it as well as a deposit of Greco-Roman myth filtered through European influence in its Museum of Fine Arts. Through repeated visits to the five labyrinthine rooms containing the eighteen tapestries, Revel makes a number of correlations between the Judeo-Christian myth of Cain and the Greek myth of Theseus. As participants in a fertility cult, for example, both men were guilty of murder; and both founded a city in its blood, Cain having founded Enock and Theseus Athens.[11] For Theseus as well as Cain, blood was the fertilizer out of which new life emerged. Revel, therefore, engages in the endeavor of drawing parallels among Theseus, Cain, and himself in an attempt to justify his own complicity in guilt, his own fear of having committed murder himself simply in knowing his desire to burn Bleston, whether he is the actual arsonist or not. In a world where the imaginary and the real change places as easily as one can change perspective, Revel is an arsonist by magical transference in burning his map of the city.

In his attempt to grasp fragments of myth and restore them to wholeness by incorporating them into his own person, to restore them to a common, meaningful center from which they must have originated, he discovered that Bleston, that "horrible amorphous town" (262) is a labyrinth that is "incomparably more bewildering than that of the Cretan palace, since it grows and alters" (195) as he explores it. Revel gradually becomes aware that Bleston is "not a city bounded by walls or avenues, standing out clearly against a background of fields, but that, like a lamp in the mist, it forms the center of a halo whose hazy fringes intermingle with those of other towns" (32-3).

Nor is it like the mythic Cretan palace whose center was fixed and accessible to the initiated. The crenelated tower of the Town Hall, which resembles "one of those lead castle keeps with which our grandparents played at toy soldiers" (51), is an anachronism, a self-condemning reminder of its medieval ancestor, the walled town in which the church stood at the center "rising out of the confused streets of the city as an oak tree does out of an oak copse, not differing in leafage, but in size and symmetry.[12]

Unlike Theseus, whose spool of thread followed him to the center of the labyrinth and then guided him safely out again, Revel's thread figuratively breaks in his hand so that his attempt "to see things clearly" becomes a futile effort, "a pretense of trying" (116). The azure sky over Crete being irrevocably lost beyond the mists of Bleston, and recoverable only on the developed film (reveler, to reveal or to develop a photo) of a travelogue, Revel decides that the only defense against entropy, "the slime and silt, the inertia and opacity of Bleston," is recognition, awareness of the doublings and triplings, the remembrance of having been some place before as a way of measuring one's progress in a labyrinth. The museum, then, as a cultural shrine dedicated to preserving the memory of the Cretan labyrinth, provides Revel with scenes whose significance he will surmise only retrospectively as he finds their doubles in his own city, his own labyrinth.

Lost in the "mud-soaked winding sheets" (120) of Bleston, Revel feels attracted to the Museum much the same as he is to the Old Cathedral. Each holds out the same hope of recovering the lost ground of his being in the rediscovered origins of myth. Worse than the condition of Ruskin, who read about the existence of "a glorious city in the Sea," and found only "a glorious city in the Mud,"[13] is the state of Revel, who sees azure skies over Crete in Bleston's movie theater, but only mud in Bleston. By retracing the journey of Theseus through the labyrinth of Crete, Revel hopes to win for himself in the labyrinth of Bleston the victory of Theseus. In the crown of light with which Ariadne armed Theseus and the clear azure that brightens Cretan skies, Revel longs to discover a ray of light breaking through Bleston's "icy stagnant waters" as he tries to transform the patterns of the Theseus tapestries of the museum into the fabric of his own life (128).

In the trees of the Cretan landscapes, for example, Revel recognizes the trees of his native France. Ann becomes Ariadne; Rose is Phaedra and then Persephone; and Lucien Blaise becomes Pirithous or Dionysus according to Revel's changing perspective. In his diary account of those brief days of sunlight, days in which he believes himself close to discovering the meaning of his own life in terms of a mythic correlation, Revel writes: "Day must be bright there, shining on the slopes of Mount Ida, along all these high peaks that pierce the sky like slow cries, glittering on the translucent waters at their feet, bathing the whole of that steep, jagged coastline, probing its ravines with long, kind sunbeams . . ." (104). As Revel continues his reverie, he employs a phrase that reads like a ritualistic chant as if to make the vision of Crete a reality in Bleston by sheer repetition of the words.

Even if Revel finally pieces the eighteen tapestries together in a story that matches the written account he later finds, such a pattern can never be superimposed on his own experience as a way of giving his own life permanent meaning. Trying to establish his own identity despite time's degenerating force, Revel seeks a connection between himself and some fixed point of reference. In spite of the many parallels Revel draws between himself and Theseus, however, he cannot close the gap that separates the Cretan Palace at Knossos from the modern city of Bleston.

The center of Crete's labyrinth finds no holding center in its modern guise. Between the azure sky over Crete and the red sky over Bleston, time's mist and fog have built a barrier beginning with Cain's City and including all that city's historical descendants: Athens, Rome, Petra, Baalbek, Timgad, or San Francisco. The "red glow of destruction reflected in the clouds" of all these cities separates them from the glue of some artist's conception of a time "when cities were still pure, beneficent and immense, when these palaces and temples were new." The conception of a never-changing city of light whose blue sky "proclaimed its permanence" (238) parallels Revel's thirst for "the elixir of immortality (307). Similarly, the tapestry artist's conception of Theseus as forever that "same young man in armor" (164) is an illusion just as it is an illusion for Revel to label James Jenkins as one kind of person, the man he met during those first days in Bleston, when people change just as circumstances do. In the labyrinth of life's experience "the detail of the pattern is movement"[14] in which everything shifts and slides beyond the possibility of fixation.

Just as it is impossible to establish a stable center, to reach a point of fixity, so is it pretentious to believe one can fix the points of one's life within a chronological sequence of past, present, and future without one point's continually impinging on another to modify it. Such patterning is possible only in the world of the imagination, the world of art and illusion. Revel's life will never fit into the tapestry's pattern, for art, like myth, is a time out of time. To perceive the pattern of one's life, to have found one's center, is to suggest that one has finished his own life's course; for in this life one cannot both be a thread in the fabric and yet to be apart from it judging the overall design.

Consequently, Revel must finally admit that his search for a center of meaning applicable to his own life in the Museum's deposit of myth is just another of his fictions, another "meaning" by which he has operated for awhile: "The pattern is complete," he reports in his diary, "and I am left out of it" (268). Revel knows that a pattern has been woven without him. James Jenkins has won Ann, and Lucien is going to marry Rose. The pattern according to which he was supposed to win Rose as his bride has consequently been broken.

As early as November, a month whose events were recalled the following June, Revel felt the attraction of a labyrinthine quest, a quest that yielded victory to Theseus, even while he feared it: "It was as though a trail had been laid for me," he writes, "at each stage of which I was allowed to see the end of the next stage, a trail that was to lead me hopelessly astray" (82). The invitation to believe that life is ordered is irresistible even though reality proves the contrary to be true. Seeking a center whose symbols can be translated into the terms of his own experience in Bleston, Revel finds remnants of culturally defined myths from times and places not his own, which are relevant to the shaping of his year in Bleston, but only as an imaginative escape from Bleston's morass of amnesia and entropy. The parallels Revel draws are often misleading in the end like his judgments concerning characters in Burton's novel whom he translates into the living citizens of Bleston, suspecting them of complicity in a murder which may only be fictional.[15]

In opposition to the sixteenth century Old Cathedral and the eighteenth century Museum with their respective murder stories depicted in art, the center (besides the commercial center which is just under construction) more immediately related to Revel's own historical time is the New Cathedral designed by E.E. Douglas, a nineteenth century architect.

Here the myth of science is enthroned in a modern-day Noah's ark or whale's skeleton, as the New Cathedral is variously called. If the Old Cathedral symbolizes the city of God having been usurped by the city of man in the symbolism of its windows, the New Cathedral represents a culmination of the city of man in an entropic city devoid of conscious symbolizing and obsessed with categorization, the latter being an emblem of modern man's compulsion to remember. The fly in capital and frieze, for example, may be the mythic Zeus, Olympian lord of the flies or it may signify Beelzebub, his infernal double. Then again flies may be culturally fictionalized as members of a class labeled Diptera.

Linguistically, the Cathedral itself may have been a temple before it was a fly, considering that Diptera derives from the Greek "dipteros" designating a temple with two "wings" of columns. A new insight for Revel is that the New Cathedral's architecture is no longer man's Bible in stone, but a museum of categorization, culture's present form of remembering, and remembrance fittingly the measure of movement in a labyrinth. As the cathedral absorbs artifacts from the city around it, drawing the city itself into it, all sense of a sacred center surrounded by a periphery radiating from it is also abolished.[16]

Revel's nightmare functions as an apocalyptic revelation of the New Cathedral's inseparability from the city's gradually increasing entropy. The dream image of the cathedral as the body of a giant fly, its nave expanding and contracting like a thorax, "its buttresses parting and closing like ribs," signifies the inevitable outcome of relegating gods and demons to the neutral zone of scientific analysis. The fly, once a symbol of immortality, either heavenly or infernal as Zeus or Beelzebub, takes its revenge in Revel's dream in the shape of "an enormous fly made of enamel and gold, its eyes of coal, its wings of quivering glass slowly opening and closing," imprisoning people and buildings alike "under the shadowy X in the transept" (288).

The image of the fly merges both city and cathedral in its eyes of Bleston coal and wings of cathedral glass. In a city where objects are no longer unchangingly symbolic or significant beyond themselves, Revel's world is one in which myth has been largely "laicized, degraded or disguised," to use the words of Joseph Campbell, who might have been commenting on Revel's experience of the New Cathedral when he described modern man's dilemma as "the situation of a man swallowed by a monster, struggling in the darkness of its belly; . . . or wandering in a labyrinth which itself is a symbol of the Infernal--and so he is in anguish . . . and can see no way out except into darkness." The labyrinth as a symbolic structure whose center encloses the beneficent powers on the inside and "forms a barrier against dreaded attacks from the outside"[17] is a definition inapplicable to the New Cathedral where inside and outside mesh beyond the lesser confusions of left and right as in the Old Cathedral.

The New Cathedral, while it appears to Burton as a plagiarism of the Old, strikes Revel as a distortion with "rare value" (126) in that the New has displaced the Old, substituting its own cultural artifacts for those of an outmoded past. Although Revel is usually misguided by his interpretations of events and their meaning, he is perceptive in viewing the two cathedrals as "two poles of an immense magnet that deflects the trajectory of all human atoms subjected to its influence according to the stuff they are made of and the energy with which they are charged" (187).

Instead of attracting, as sanctuaries by definition should, since they symbolically participate in the primordial act of creating and consequently the sacred character of that act, the twin cathedrals deflect humanity from their centers, which have been deconsecrated by the act of murder, a form of defilement.

Perhaps death with a purpose, the mythic creed of death as sacrifice necessary for new life, is the distinct difference symbolized by Cain in the Old Cathedral and that is lost in the New where death is blatant murder without intent to revitalize, an act of the fittest surviving. The New Cathedral is a travesty of its medieval prototype, which attempted in its imagery "to embody the whole of Christian knowledge, theological, moral, natural, and historical."[18] In place of a Bible in stone, the nineteenth century has erected an architectural *Origin of Species*.

The cathedral's emphasis on the lowest forms of organic life, according to Darwin's classification, parallels Revel's vision of the city itself, the shape of which he compares to that of an egg and which he calls variously a larva, an amoeba, a hydra, and a tortoise. On another scale he talks about its cats, wolves, foxes, bisons, zebras, rams, bulls, bears, and monkeys, or its birds like pheasants, cranes, and falcons.

The New Cathedral, which is the city's model, is, in summary, "the epitome of all things Blestonian."[19] Altogether the cathedral is not very different from the city's university museum with its "stuffed animals" (232) and Zoo with its cages of "listless wild beasts" (236) in Pleasance Gardens. The frozen creatures decorating the cathedral capital are mobilized again over and in the city streets where "clouds part in ragged streamers, like an octopus's tentacles" and "cats stretch themselves on every doorstep" (147). Fearful of the inescapability of his plight in Bleston, which is all the more deadening for being many cities (only "bits of wasteland" separating one from another, hence suggesting every city), Revel calls it "that hydra, that octopus with spreading tentacles, the squid disgorging its black ink" (255) over him and its citizens so that they no longer recognize themselves or each other, an amnesia Revel is neurotic about falling into himself.

In short, the whole classification of animals which forms the body of the New Cathedral is paralleled in the city's organic system. From its caged beasts to its vermin "alive or dead, spectacular or parasitic, meat or carrion" (304), Revel sees the city's powers as incarnate in them.

The significance of all these energy levels coming together and obliterating distinctions between dead and alive, is that the New Cathedral extends and participates in the city's amorphous nature rather than serves as a center whose original intent betokened man's attempt to transcend time and mortality through the preservation of myths and immortality.

While the zoological classification of the New Cathedral is least successful in its representation of man, its reproduction of the fly is "a very fine one" (131), making one of the lowest forms of life more nearly perfect than man, who has been reduced to the level of one of the lowest. Not surprisingly in this magnet of a building that deflects rather than attracts, the flies inside mirror those without. Revel compares himself to a fly crawling across a curtain as he prowls "over the town's surface" (48) in search of a room to rent. Likewise, Burton (anagram for Butor), his surrogate father who reveals to Revel through his novel the plagiarism of Bleston's New Cathedral, is plagued by flies first in his hospital room and then in his home.

In the hospital where he is recovering from an "accident," Burton is helpless to protect himself against "the buzzing flight of a huge fly" that lands on his forehead, "sucking the drops of sweat with its tiny proboscis" (183), an invasion suggesting a reversal of roles, flies being superior to man. Later, convalescing in his home after being dismissed from the hospital, Burton's eye begins "to follow a fly wheeling about in the sunbeams" in the room where his wife and Revel are visiting him, and finally, completely distraught, he overturns his tea tray leaving "a great dripping stain on the white sheet" (228). Either Revel is just paranoid in his quest to invent a conspiracy, or flies have usurped the place and significance of man himself.

Like Revel, who draws symbolic parallels between myth and himself, the reader of *Passing Time* is tempted to draw parallels between Sartre's *The Flies* and Butor's novel. The flies that surround Zeus, who is himself The Fly as their lord, and those in pursuit of Orestes, are an image of man himself reduced to the level of an insect. Inside the city's religious center, once regarded as sacred, as well as without, Bleston is fly-infested.

Mrs. Jenkins, who once had posed as a living model for two of the Cathedral's sculptures, wears a ring enclosing a fly in a glass bubble, a haunting talisman that links her to the cathedral which she has incorporated into herself by having made her father, who was its architect, "her Pygmalion" from whom "she had slowly appropriated all that she could of the glances and curves and graces that he had sculptured in stone" (175). Bleston's daughter as well, Mrs. Jenkins levels in herself the high and the low, combining in herself the Ladies Astronomy and Botany (160, 175). In her, hierarchies are reduced to entropic monotony. As Revel intensifies his assault on the life-sucking creatures of Bleston, Mrs. Jenkins, always cold in her associations with him, fixes her gaze more frequently and intently on the fly frozen in the glass bubble. Like the fly in the bubble, Mrs. Jenkins is an image of Bleston's frozen state, its state of continual change, but change without meaning.

Like the New Cathedral's flies which deflect the city's truth back onto itself, the tortoise mimics man's fall from Promethean heights into entropic mud. Revel knows that "under their carapaces of fatigue and resigned acceptance" (296) Bleston's inhabitants long for the city's death as much as he does. While the Promethean flame has not quite burned out, Bleston is like an impenetrable carapace within which "a slow relentless flame" issues, but which burns too slowly to transform the city's "sand to glass" (307). Overrun by these mud creatures, Bleston has no center from which they are excluded.

Looking at the Old Cathedral, that replica of man's self enthronement, Revel observes that even its facade glistens under a thin carapace of ice. Continuing the process of degeneracy, the New Cathedral, which inherited the essence of the Old in receiving its bells, assumes in its entirety the shape of a tortoise in the sketch Revel draws in the margin of his copy of *The Bleston Murder* beside the words "New Cathedral" (150). Recalling the events in his diary, Revel writes:

> I drew a tiny picture of a tortoise, promptly wondering why, among all the animals I had seen that day, all of which were represented by a carving on one of the capitals in that building, I had chosen that particular one (150).

The drawing reflects Revel's gradual identification with the city he despises and writes about as a way of escape. Like Bleston itself which has no limits, which spreads like a cancerous growth and diffuses itself like an amoeba, the tortoise, as a kind of city mascot, penetrates into all the city's areas reducing all to the same level of plodding apathy characteristic of itself.

In the Museum, too, Revel's attention is drawn to "the huge tortoise surrounded by torn shreds of human flesh" (161). the tortoise as symbolic of the merging of centers into an amorphous conglomerate intrudes into one of Revel's nighttime visions in which he sees the tortoise with the appendages of wings, armor, and horns hovering over his bed. As synecdoches for the fly, the tortoise, and the bull, these images, in turn, all meld into symbols of Bleston with its cultural/religious centers and Revel himself as a dweller therein. In his diary Revel fixes the memory:

> . . . all night, unable to sleep, without a moment's respite from the tormenting breath of the creature that seemed to hover a few inches above me on enormous fly's wings, a monstrous tortoise with scales of cast iron and brick, horned like a bull, its muzzle stained with smoky blood (256).

To locate a geographical and historical axis in such a place and state of blurred physical and psychological boundaries is a quest doomed to failure from the start, like Revel's similar attempt to draw boundaries around time by laying out events in perfect chronological order in his diary without infiltrations from the past or projections into the future confounding that preconceived order. Unable to rid himself or Bleston of this creature's threatening presence (carnivorous as it is depicted in the Museum tapestry), Revel copes by describing its size as it changes from place to place; the tortoise in the New Cathedral being, he writes, "as huge compared to the living tortoise I had seen the previous Sunday in Pleasance Gardens as was the latter compared to the one I had drawn on my copy of *The Bleston Murder*, and yet small compared to that tortoise which I had determined to go and look at the next day, that monstrous, carnivorous tortoise in the third tapestry of the Museum" (158).

This scrupulous attention devoted to a comparative analysis of physical dimensions is matched by Revel's careful recording of the changing size of the Acropolis (an ancient labyrinth itself)[20] in the background of the tapestries from one scene to another. Detail in general is a necessary part of Revel's tactics against the fear of losing his memory, his fear of growing progressively more forgetful, which is the psychological counterpart of physical entropy. As the red layers of cloud merge with the red silt of the land, Revel finds it increasingly more urgent for him to uncover Bleston's original soil and the ground of his own being as well.

But the new center which finally does emerge out of this city's peat bog is "a new commercial spire intruding into the life of Bleston's inhabitants, distorting the entire city" with its "huge wall of gleaming bricks, too sure a proof of the evil city's vitality, a token of change canceling all hope of genuine change" (241). Revel seems to hear this new facade boasting of its "hydra head" on a "vast carapace" (241), a monster he will not be able to destroy. Inability to control Bleston's architectural oozings in the shape of yet another pseudo-center baffles Revel in this city where "cells reproduce themselves" (241).

Although the city's face is constantly changing and its centers elusive and shifting, Revel discovers a partial anodyne against Bleston's "gigantic, insidious sorcery" (27) in Horace Buck. An outsider like himself, Buck has subconsciously found a way of surviving by following Bleston's revolving fair, its remnant of a spiritual nucleus. Traveling around the fringes of Bleston's central business district, the fair is a "miniature mobile town" that has retained, at least fragmentarily, the characteristics of a cultic sacred center. In the bear hunt, for instance, the fair re-enacts a kind of fertility cult in which the bear must sacrifice its life in order that the prize of new life may be regained.[21] A follower of the fair, the remnant of an ancient, pagan fire festival, Buck is drawn to the hunt, "that tiny theater in which, against a forest background, a brown wooden bear rears up and growls and his eyes flash, while the number of hits scored is registered on the glass facade of the booth" (109-10). In this game Buck is more skilled than all the others.

At the fair, too, all classes of society gather together in a relaxation of tension and of social class barriers. At the fair, then, Buck the outcast mingles with the city's elite, with Burton, Lucien, Jenkins, and the Bailey sisters. The fair as a remnant of the religious festival of ancient times, preserves, if only fragmentarily, a re-enactment of the primordial creation, "a passage to the great age, the moment when men stop their activity in order to gain access to the reservoir of all-powerful and ever elemental forces represented by the primordial age."[22] The goal of rebirth has been lost, however, even though Buck knows a little of debauchery and excess (characteristic of the ritual festival) in his women and liquor. Not surprisingly for this labyrinthine city of reversals, the man whom Revel calls his savior is the man Revel's landlady labels as one of "'those black devils'" (111).

Horace, surviving on the city's fringes, welcomes Revel when he is still a stranger, finds a home for him when the city's "Anchor" becomes unbearable, breaks bread with him in a city that provides no true nourishment, and gives Revel "spirits" when Bleston offers only a tasteless fare of bland liquids: tea, mineral water, soda, orangeade . . . (9). In contrast to the city's external fires, which are "mechanical, corrupting, and destroying," Buck offers Revel alcoholic drinks, whose internal fire is "spermatic, generative, reopening." In the company of the drinking Horace, Revel experiences "a communion of life and of fire."[23] And as they drink, alcohol's power to "create mental potentialities" is loosened. Only Buck is able to understand and share Revel's frustration with the city. Acknowledging his indebtedness to Horace, Revel confesses:

> This was already a first awakening; I believe that Horace Buck is well aware of the extent of the service he did me at that time, for in his innocent unfathomable gaze are hidden depths . . . he knows that he has, so to speak, saved my life, rescued that consciousness in me . . . which, though sick and soiled, is still alive in me and is now groping its way toward health and daylight (116).

For Buck the labyrinth of Bleston is a playground like the "small maze" Revel discovers in one of the city parks. For Revel, on the other hand, his maze is neither a playground nor built on the model of the one that Theseus threaded; rather, it is turned inside out where life on the shaggy fringes of Bleston approaches a state of significance lost in the city's former centers. Whereas "the center would seem to be the clear and comforting abode of the pure, and the periphery the dark and disquieting abode of the impure,"²⁴ Revel experiences the reverse as closer to the truth when he reviews his days in Bleston.

Familiar with the traveling fair, Buck also frequents the city's Amusement Arcade opposite the Town Hall where it serves as "a miniature replica in the center of town, or that great permanent amusement park in Pleasance Gardens, in the 12th district" (135). To even further complicate the possibility of finding one major center, Pleasance Gardens is a mirror image of the Old Cathedral which, in turn, is already confused in Revel's mind with the New Cathedral. Observing Pleasance Gardens for the first time, Revel notes its "monumental entrance gates whose two square towers, adorned with grimy stucco, are crowned, like that edifice (temple or mosque?) dominating Cain's city in the Window, with two enormous yellow-half-moons attached to lightning conductors . . ." (148).

Like the New Cathedral, Pleasance Gardens vaunts a Zoo with animals classified and caged according to genus and species. Unlike the fair, however, of which it is a distorted imitation, the Garden's "big, cheap restaurants," themselves a mimicry of eating as a religious act, are empty and its entrance gate "is armored as if to protect a safe and only opens on great occasions and for important processions" (148). Formerly a cultural center, Pleasance Gardens is now an empty center.

The fair still contains the remnants of a religious ritual. The church feasts, on the other hand, are all like that of All Saints Day, "the feast of the dead" (66) as Revel calls it. Christmas, Easter, and New Year's Day, once the feastdays of life, light, and renewal placing man in accord with seasonal changes, are observed in Bleston by locked doors, empty restaurants, and a general atmosphere of darkness. On Christmas Day, for example, the city's Amusement Arcade is the only place open and the bells heard from without mingle their sound with the clangor of the bells from within as "merely those of the Town Hall clock tower" (189) reminding Horace and Revel that they are hungry on this feast of the Bread of Life. Easter, too, is a "ghost of a dead festival," for while the city's stores display "greeting cards, beribboned and bespangled, adorned with chicks and rabbits and bells" (253), the park which bears the holiday's name, Easter Park, contains "beds of withered flowers" with "rotting petals and crumpled leaves" (296). New Year's, a pagan feast "destined to reinvigorate existence and restore the cohesion of social life,"[25] is reduced to a display of fireworks for Bleston's citizens and a night of drinking for Buck and Revel, both activities proving to be ineffectual attempts to renew life.

Even the fair, which preserves some remnants of the sacred if only in the form of amusement, is being consumed by "the city center" (294) around which it revolves. This "little traveling town," this "village of canvas and wood and painted metal" is only "seemingly nomadic" (144) since it adheres to Bleston's egg-shaped orbit as it revolves around Bleston's inner core. It, too, shares the wasteland as a "rent in the fabric of the city" to which Bleston's citizens come only as prowlers "spying out the novelties and changes" (146). Those changes, however, are like the ones bursting out of its New Cathedral, which are not genuine but mere excrescences.

Revel's search for a spacial center coincident with his need for a spiritual one is like the quest of the alchemist who uses fire as a purifying agent to release the gold lodged in abandoned rubbish: "I see the gleam of a precious raw material," he writes in September about that same month's experience, "from which I can make gold; but how deep I must plunge to reach it, what efforts I must make to secure and collect all that dust" (281).

Consonant with *Passing Time*, Jung calls alchemy "a cathedral built for things," and describes its value as an attempt to recover a "psychic content lost and abandoned by the time of the search."[26] Revel partially succeeds in his battle against forgetfulness, not by remembrance, but rather in his recognition of failure. In the words of one critic, *Passing Time* "is a recognition of defeat, but one where the emphasis falls on the word 'recognition' and not on 'defeat'."[27] As Revel prepares to leave Bleston at the end of his year there, he packs up his "pitiful accumulation of futile phrases, like the ruins of an unfinished building . . . " (262).

But while the phrases may have been futile attempts at discovering a center of meaning, they have succeeded in striking several recognitions. Consequently, 'defeat' may be too harsh a word to use. Although Revel's achievement may impress him as minuscule, the diary has served him as a partial defense against oblivion. And for the reader, Revel's diary is a guide into one's own labyrinthine search for meaning just as Burton's novel introduced Revel to Bleston and helped him pass the time while there.

Bleston's cancerous growth continues in spite of the fires Revel may have set, fires whose purpose was to destroy only so that the work of purification might begin, a purification signaled by initial destruction. Although Revel partially frees himself from his prison of amnesia and manages to escape from the city with an incomplete journal of its entropic forces, he loses both Ann and Rose, especially Rose whom he calls "my Rose blossoming in this marshland, among its creeping miasmas . . . elusive, reserved, lively, simple-hearted, tender and cruel Rose" (217).

By continually trying to weave his life into contexts of meaning, Revel has lost the sense of living in the present moment; he has lost his ability to love without calculation, to respond spontaneously to the moment. Even though he has lost both of the Bailey sisters, Revel has his journal. Fragmentary as it is, with distortions, modifications, and misinterpretations, Revel's diary is the thread that finally brings him through the labyrinth of Bleston with his life. Because he has written it for Ann, she can still be seen in a sense as his Ariadne, the reason for this rope of language stretched temporally from the beginning to the end of his stay in Bleston.

Because he could tell the story of his year he was able "to change senseless misery into significant doom."[28] In other words, the mere act of telling the story about himself as Theseus has preserved Revel's life by allowing him to transform a year of condemnation in an inferno into a quest for meaning even though that meaning is only fragmentary and changing.

Revel is not unlike Scheherazade, who found life in telling stories. Using language as a way of reversing a situation from bad to bearable by a mere change of perspective is a maneuver both characteristic and lawful in the game of labyrinthine questing. That game, however, extends beyond narrative and text to include the reader. Because we experience Bleston completely through what Revel chooses to relate, the Bleston we are given is necessarily a distorted one, filtered through Revel's mind as he sees it.

Butor, as the voice behind Revel, must know another one, and different from both is the mental construct the reader builds as he reads and recreates his own Bleston. Ultimately, Bleston is a mere pretext for the endless number of texts that grow out of it. Like Burton reading Bleston, and Revel reading Bleston through Burton, every reader and writer is a detective, searching futilely through a common body of filtered evidence for the clue that will unlock the mystery and meaning of life that will reveal a center giving orientation to labyrinthine confusion.

Notes

1. Joseph Campbell, *Myths To Live By* (New York: The Viking Press, 1972), p.22]

2. Victor Hugo, *Notre Dame de Paris*, trans. M. Dupres (New York: Beechhurst Press, 1949), p.141

3. Michel Butor, *Passing Time*, trans. Jean Stewart (New York: Simon and Schuster, 1960), p.4. All subsequent references to this edition will be noted parenthetically within the text.

4. Mircea Eliade, *Myths, Dreams, and Mysteries*, trans. Philip Mairet (New York: Harper and Row, 1967), p.34

5. S.H. Hooke, ed., *The Labyrinth: Further Studies in the Relation Between Myth and Ritual in The Ancient World* (New York: Macmillan Co., 1935). According to Hooke, "the monster is the ancient dying and the rising god, the slain and the living king, the symbol of the price that must ever be paid for the gift of life" (Intro. p.ix). "Above all, the labyrinth was the centre of activities concerned with those greatest of mysteries, Life and Death. There men tried by every means known to them to overcome death and renew life" p.42.

6. Standish Meacham, "The Church In the Victorian City," *Victorian Studies*, II (1968), p.376

7. John Ruskin, *The Stones of Venice* (New York: Charles E. Merrill and Co., 1891), p.156

8. Ruskin, p.181

9. Gertrude Jobes, *Dictionary of Mythology, Folklore, and Symbols* (New York: Scarecrow Press, 1961), p.1089

10. For a full treatment of the theme see Jean Seznec, *The Survival of the Pagan Gods*, trans. Barbara Sessions (Princeton: Princeton University Press, 1972)

11. Hook, *Middle Eastern Mythology* (Baltimore: Penguin Books, 1963), p.126. "Thus the original form of the first part of Yahwist's story of Cain and Abel, namely, that contained in 4:1-15 was probably a ritual myth depicting a ritual slaying by the flight of the slayer, who was protected by a mark which indicated his sacred character." Philippe Borgeaud, "The Open Entrance to the Closed Palace of the King,"

History of Religions, 14 (August 1974), p.17. "The young people he [Theseus] brings back from Crete after his victory will be the citizens of the new city he founds. By bringing about the synoecism . . . Theseus becomes in effect the true founder of cultural Athens."

12. Ruskin, p.155

13. Ruskin, xii

14. T.S. Eliot, *Four Quartets*, "Burnt Norton," IV

15. Similarities that exist between the fictional murderer's house and that of one of Bleston's citizens are not sufficient evidence upon which to convict a man, especially in a city where parallels, mirrors, and false identities are excessive. Whether Hamilton/Burton is exposing an actual fratricide in *The Bleston Murder* is a question never finally answered in *Passing Time*.

16. Eliade, pp.33, 237

17. Roger Caillois, *Man and the Sacred*, trans. Meyer Barash (Glencoe, Illinois: The Free Press, 1959), p.53

18. E. Panofsky, *Gothic Architecture and Scholasticism* (Elnora, New York: Meridian, 1951), p.44

19. Thomas O'Donnell, "The Alchemist in the Labyrinth: A Joycean Approach to Michel Butor," Diss. University of Wisconsin 1971, p. 179

20. C.N. Deedes, "The Labyrinth" in *The Labyrinth*, S.H. Hooke, ed., p.30

21. A whole dissertation has been devoted to a comparison of Faulkner and Butor in which McWilliams notes the importance of the wilderness hunt as a religious ritual in both Faulkner's *The Bear, Man, and God* and Butor's *Passing Time*. David Dean McWilliams, "The Influence of William Faulkner on Michel Butor," Diss. University of Oregon, 1969

22. Caillois, p.59

23. Gaston Bachelard, *The Psychoanalysis of Fire*, trans. A.C.M. Ross (Boston: Beacon Press, 1968), pp.73-87

24. Caillois, p.52

25. Caillois, p.110

26. Carl Jung, *Man and His Symbols* (New York: Doubleday and Co., 1964), p.253

27. John Sturrock, *The French New Novel: Claude Simon, Michel Butor, Alain Robbe-Grillet* (London: Oxford University Press, 1969) p.152

28. Arnold Weinstein, *Modern Fiction Studies* (Paris: Gallimard Press, 1970), p.51

29. Leon Roudiez, *French Fiction Today* (New Brunswick: Rutgers University Press, 1972). "Every writer is Scheherazade, every writer harbors within himself a threat of death . . . both within himself and about himself. The threat that lies outside of him corrodes him, so to speak, internally . . . The writer, in speaking will at once remove the threat of death that weighs upon him, and, of course, also weighs on the entire future of society" p.283.

Afterword

For Brontë, Dickens, and Hardy, as for others in the nineteenth century, the city seems fallen because, while its church may still function as the city's chief landmark, it does not draw its citizens to itself as the source and end of meaningful activity. It does not mirror a cosmic order, or the voice of divine authority. Instead, city and church conflict in ideology with each other. In *Villette* the tension is portrayed primarily in psychological terms. For Lucy Snowe the church's authority, too restrictive and reclusive, is countered by the city's, too permissive and diffusive. Her solution, therefore, is retreat without completely abandoning the ideal of either church or city.

Although Dickens also imparts human psychology to the architectural structures that enclose its members, he portrays Cloisterham in its temporal dynamic as well. Because the first city was a necropolis out of which rose expressions of faith in eternal life, it is appropriate that Cloisterham be a boneyard, helpless in its present state to declare the "Resurrection and the Life." Immersed in the timelessness of past history and the timelessness of present stagnation, Cloisterham stands in need of deliverance from this limbo, a limbo transformed into a hell for Revel in *Passing Time*. Like Ezekiel's dry bones inspired through the union of human willing and divine grace, Cloisterham shows promise of a coming resurrection by a like concurrence of guilt removed and the demonic exorcised, a reunion of city and church.

By the end of the century, however, city and church (defined as one entity in such names as Cloisterham and Christminster) are irreconcilably divorced from one another in the values each has come to represent. The irony of the situation is only emphasized by allusions to a New Jerusalem, a veritable city of God wed to the City of Man, a city envisioned Biblically as a bride adorned for her husband who will be God Himself. In its very name, Christminster mocks what it supposedly signifies.

In the first three novels considered, the idea of a hierarchically ordered universe, with a center that gives orientation to all that emanates from it, becomes a highly questioned assumption, a remote possibility, and finally an absurd presumption. The dynamics of the labyrinth itself, as a kind of city prototype, is gradually perceived, not as a complex system leading eventually to a center of rebirth, but as an inescapable disorder without center. Proust, for example, was recalling an idyllic past when he described Combray's church as "epitomizing the town, representing it, speaking of it and for it to the horizon."[1] The time is gone when medieval ramparts enclose a cluster of houses around a church forming a circular harmony.

By mid-twentieth century, one can find a culminating expression of the theme in Michel Butor's *Passing Time (L'Emploi du Temps)*, a novel in which labyrinth and city coalesce, both symbolic of man's search for a center of meaning in an infinitely complex universe. Seen through the eyes of an outsider, Jacques Revel, the labyrinthine city of Bleston baffles any previously held theory of the city as a foreshadowing of the Heavenly Jerusalem or as a labyrinth wherein the properly initiated experience rebirth. Both concepts are exposed as culturally sustained illusions, though perhaps necessary for man's sanity.

Notes

1. Marcel Proust, "Swann's Way" from *Remembrance of Things Past,* trans. C.K. Scott Moncrieff (New York: Modern Library, 1928), p.59

Bibliography of Works Cited

Adams, Henry. *Monte-Saint-Michel and Chartres*. Garden City, New York: Doubleday and Co., 1959

Allcroft, A. Hadrian. *The Circle and the Cross*. 2 vols. London: Macmillan and Co., 1930

Allott, Miriam, Ed. *The Brontës: The Critical Heritage*. London: Routledge and Kegan Paul, 1974

Alvarez, A. "Jude the Obscure." In *Hardy: A Collection of Critical Essays*. Ed. Albert Guerard. Englewood Cliffs: Prentice-Hall, 1963.

Apollodorus, *The Library*. 2 vols. Trans. James Frazer. London: William Heinemann, 1921

Aries, Philippe, *Western Attitudes Toward Death: From the Middle Ages to the Present*. Trans. Patricia M. Ranum. Baltimore: Johns Hopkins University Press, 1974

Arnold Matthew. *Complete Prose Works*. Ed. R.H. Super. Ann Arbor: University of Michigan Press, 1960

Auden, W.H. "The Guilty Vicarage: Notes on the Detective Story." *Harper Magazine*, 196 (May 1948), 406-412

Auerback, Nina. "Charlotte Brontë: The Two Countries." *University of Toronto Quarterly*, 42 (1972-73), 336-7

Austen, Jane. *Mansfield Park*. Ed. John Lucas. new York: Oxford University Press, 1970

Austen, Jane. *Northanger Abbey*. London: R. Bentley, 1833

Bachelard, Gaston. *The Psychoanalysis of Fire*. Trans. A.C.M. Ross. Boston: Beacon Press, 1968

Beyle, Marie-Henri (Stendhal). *The Red and the Black*, Trans. C.K. Scott-Moncrieff. New York: Modern Library, 1926

Bonney, T.G. Ed. *Cathedrals, Abbeys, and Churches of England and Wales*. London: Cassell and Co., 1891

Borgeaud, Philippe. "The Open Entrance to the Closed Palace of the King: The Greek Labyrinth in Context." *History of Religions*, 14 (August 1974), 17

Brontë, Charlotte. *Villette*. New York: Harper and Brothers, 1899

Brontë, Emily. *Wuthering Heights*. Ed. H.W. Garrod. London: Oxford University Press, 1932

Brown, Charles Brockden. *Wieland or the Transformation, Together with Memoirs of Carwin the Biloquist: A Fragment*. Ed. Fred L. Pattee. New York: Harcourt, Brace and Co., 1926

Bumpus, Thomas F. *The Cathedrals of England and Wales*. London: T. Werner Laurie, 1921. Pl. St. Paul's Cathedral, 96. Pl. Rochester Cathedral, 88

Bunyan, John. *Pilgrim's Progress: From This World to That Which Is to Come*. New York: Heritage Press, 1942

Burkhard, Charles. "The Nuns of *Villette*." *The Victorian Newsletter*, 44 (Fall, 1973), 10

Butler, Alban, Ed. *The Lives of the Saints*, Vol.6. New York: P.J. Kennedy and Sons, 1937

Butor, Michel. *Passing Time*. Trans. Jean Stewart. new York: Simon and Schuster, 1960

Butler, Samuel. *The Way of All Flesh*. London: Oxford University Press, 1936

Caillois, Roger. *Man and the Sacred*. Trans. Meyer Barash. Glencoe: The Free Press, 1959

Campbell, Joseph. *Myths to Live By*. New York: Viking Press, 1972

Carden, Percy. *The Murder of Edwin Drood*. Intro. B.W. Matz. London: Cecil Palmer, 1920. Plates of Jasper's Gatehouse

Carlyle, Thomas. *Sartor Resartus*. New York: E.P. Dutton and Co., 1916

Clough, Arthur. *Poems*. Ed. H.F. Lowry, A.L.P. Norrington, and F.L. Mulhauser. New York: Oxford University Press, 1952

Coulanges, Fustel de. *The Ancient City: A Study on the Religion, Laws, and Institutions of Greece and Rome*. Trans. Willard Small. Boston: Lee Shephard, 1874

Dickens, Charles. *Bleak House*. London: J.M. Dent, 1954

Dickens, Charles. *Dombey and Son*. Harmondsworth: Penguin, 1970

Dickens. *Great Expectations*. New York: Dutton, 1950

Dickens. *The Mystery of Edwin Drood*. New York: New American Library, 1961

Dickinson, Robert E. *The West European City: A Geographical Interpretation.* London: Routledge and Kegan Paul, 1973

Dostoevsky, Fodor. *Notes from the Underground.* New York: New American Library, 1961

Dyos, H.J. and Wolff, Michael, ed. *The Victorian City.* 2 vols. London: Routledge and Kegan Paul, 1973

Eliade, Mircea. *Myths, Dreams, and Mysteries.* Trans. Philip Miaret. New York: Harper and Row, 1967

Eliade. *The Sacred and the Profane: The Nature of Religion.* Trans. Willard Trask. New York: Harcourt Brace, 1959

Eliot, George. *Middlemarch.* Ed. G.S. Haight. Boston: Houghton Mifflin, 1956

Fiedler, Leslie. *Love and Death in the American Novel.* Rev. ed. New York: Dell Publishing Co., 1966

Flaubert, Gustave. *Madame Bovary.* Trans. Francis Steegmuller. New York: Random House, 1957

Frederic, Harold. *The Damnation of Theron Ware or The Illumination.* Ed. Everett Carter. Cambridge: Belknap Press of Harvard University Press, 1960

Gadd, George F. "Datchery, the Enigma: The Case for Tartar." *Dickensian* 2 (Jan. 1906) 13-16. Also "The History of a Mystery: A Review of the Solutions to 'Edwin Drood!" *Dickensian* 1 (Sept. Oct. Nov. Dec. 1905) 240-244, 270-274, 293-297, 320-323. Plate of Gatehouse 3 (March 1906) 64

Gerin, Winifred. *Charlotte Brontë: The Evolution of Genius.* London: Oxford University Press, 1967

Graves, Robert. *The Greek Myths.* 2 vols. Edinburgh: R. and R. Clark, 1955

Graves, Robert and Ratai, Raphael. *Hebrew Myths: The Book of Genesis.* New York: Doubleday and Co., 1964

Gutkind, E.A. *Urban Development in Western Europe: France and Belgium.* New York: Free Press, 1970, 41

Hardy, Thomas. *Jude the Obscure.* New York: Crowell-Collier Co., 1962

Hardy, Thomas. *The Writings of Thomas Hardy in Prose and Verse* Vol. 18. Anniversary Edition. New York: Harper and Brothers, 1898

Hawthorne, Nathaniel. *The Marble Faun.* Ed. Ernest Rhys. London: J.M. Dent and Sons, 1920

Heilman, Robert. "Charlotte Brontë and the Moon." *Nineteenth Century Fiction*, 14 (March 1960), 296-97.

Hofmann, Werner. *The Earthly Paradise: Art in the Nineteenth Century.* New York: George Braziller, 1961

Hooke, S.H. ed. *The Labyrinth: Further Studies in the Relation between Myth and Ritual in the Ancient World.* New York: Macmillan Co., 1935

Hooke. *Middle Eastern Mythology.* Baltimore: Penguin, 1963

Howells, William Dean. *A Hazard of New Fortunes.* New York: Harper, 1911

Howells. *The Leatherwood God.* New York: Century Co., 1916

Howells. *A Modern Instance.* Boston: Houghton Mifflin, 1909

Howells. *The Rise of Silas Lapham.* London: Oxford University Press, 1948

Hugo, Victor. *Notre Dame de Paris.* Trans. M. Dupres. New York: Beechhurst Press, 1949

James, Henry. *The American.* 2 vols. New York: Scribner's, 1935

James, Henry. *The Bostonians.* Ed. I. Howe. New York: Modern Library, 1956

James, Henry. *Portrait of a Lady.* Ed. Robert D. Bamberg. New York: Scribner's and Sons, 1923

Jobes, Gertrude. *Dictionary of Mythology, Folklore, and Symbols.* New York: Scarecrow Press, 1961, 1889

Johnson, E.D.H. "'Daring the Dread Glance'" Charlotte Brontë's Treatment of the Supernatural in *Villette*." *Nineteenth Century Fiction*, 20 (1966) 325-335

Jung, Carl. *Man and His Symbols.* Garden City, New York: Doubleday and Co., 1964

Keats, John. "Verse Letter to J.H. Reynolds, 25 March 1818." *Letters of John Keats*, Ed. Robert Gittings. London: Oxford University Press, 1970

Kuntz, Paul G. "The Labyrinth." *Thought: A Review of Culture and Idea,* 47 (Spring 1972) 5-15

Lawrence, D.H. *The Rainbow.* New York: B.W. Heubsch, 1922

Levy, Gertrude R. *The Gate of Horn: A Study of Religious Conceptions of the Stone Age, and Their Influence upon European Thought.* London: Faber and Faber, 1948

Lewis, Matthew (Monk). *The Monk.* Ed. Louis Peck. New York: Grove Press, 1959

Lynch, Kevin. *The Image of the City.* Cambridge: M.I.T. Press, 1964

Matthews, W.H. *Mazes and Labyrinths: A General Account of Their History and Development.* London: Longmans, Green and Co., 1922

Meacham, Standish. "The Church in the Victorian City." *Victorian Studies,* 11 (1968), 359-78

Miller, J. Hillis. *The Disappearance of God: Five Nineteenth Century Writers.* Cambridge: Belknap Press of Harvard University Press, 1963

Miller, J. Hillis. *Thomas Hardy: Distance and Desire.* Cambridge: Belknap Press of Harvard University Press, 1970

Bibliography of Works Consulted

Albright, W.F. *Yahweh and the Gods of Canaan: A Historical Analysis of Two Contrasting Faiths.* Garden City, New York: Doubleday, 1968

Auden, W.H. *The Enchafed Flood; or, The Romantic Iconography of the Sea.* New York: Random House, 1950

Aylmer, Felix. *The Drood Case.* London: Rupert Hart-Davis, 1964

Ayrton, Michael. *The Maze Maker.* London: Longmans Green, and Co., 1967

Baird, James. *Ishmael,* Chap.14 "The Infernal City." Baltimore: Johns Hopkins Press, 1956

Baker, Richard. *The Drood Murder Case.* Berkeley: University of California Press, 1951

Becker, Ernest. *The Denial of Death.* New York: Collier Macmillan, 1973

Betjeman, John. *Victorian and Edwardian London.* London: B.T. Batsford, 1969, ix-xi

Briggs, Asa. *Victorian Cities.* New York: Harper Row, 1965

British Broadcasting Corporation. *Ideas and Beliefs of the Victorians: An Historic Revaluation of the Victorian Age.* 1950

Burrows, Ronald M. *The Discoveries in Crete: And Their Bearing on the History of Ancient Civilization.* London: John Murray, 1908

Butor, Michel. Inventory: *Essays,* Ed. Richard Howard. London: Jonathan Cape, 1968

Chadwick, Owen. *The Victorian Church. Parts I and II.* London: A.C. Black, 1966

Dauster, Frank. "Notes on Borges' Labyrinths." *Hispanic Review,* 30 (April 1962), 142-148

Drummond, Andrew. *The Church in English Fiction.* Leicester: Edgar Backus, 1952

Dunbar, Georgia S. "Proper Names in *Villette.*" *Nineteenth Century Fiction,* 15 (1960), 77-80

Encyclopedia of World Art. Vols VIII and XI. London: McGraw-Hill, 1962

Ferguson, George. *Signs and Symbols in Christian Art.* New York: Oxford University Press, 1954., 13-22

Fildes, Luke. "The Mysteries of Edwin Drood." *Dickensian,* 1 (Dec. 1905) 319-21

Forster, John. *The Life of Charles Dickens.* Vol.3. London: Chapman and Hall, 1872-74

Fortuna, Diane De Turo. "The Labyrinth of Art: Myth and Ritual in James Joyce's *A Portrait of the Artist as a Young Man.*" Diss. Johns Hopkins University, 1667

Gaskell, E.C. *The Life of Charlotte Brontë.* Ed. Temple Scott and B.S. Willette, 1858; rpt. London: Downey and Co., 1901

Grimsditch, Herbert B. *Character and Environment in the Novels of Thomas Hardy.* New York: Haskell House, 1966

Hamilton, Edith. *Mythology: Timeless Tales of Gods and Heroes.* New York: New American Library, 1942

Heppenstall, Rayner. "The Novels of Michel Butor," *The London Magazine,* 4 (July, 1963)

Inglis, K.S. *Churches and the Working Classes in Victorian England.* London: Routledge and Kegan Paul, 1963

Jackson, Henry J. *About Edwin Drood.* New York: Haskell House, 1974

Langton, Robert. *Charles Dickens and Rochester.* 4th ed. Rochester: T. Oldroyd, 1888. Plates of gatehouse

Larue, Gerald A. *Ancient Myth and Modern Man.* Englewood Cliffs: Prentice-Hall, 1975

Lewis, C.S. *The Discarded Image.* Cambridge: Harvard University Press, 1964

Maison, Margaret. *The Victorian Vision: Studies in the Religious Novel.* New York: Sheed and Ward, 1961

Marx, Leo. *The Machine in the Garden: Technology and the Pastoral Ideal in America.* New York: Oxford University Press, 1964

Mazzola, Lars Charles. "Labyrinthos: The Animal as Generative Center in the Life and Work of James Joyce." Dissertation, University of Minnesota, 1974

Murillo, L.A. "The Labyrinthos of Jorge Luis Borges: An Introductory to the Stories of The Aleph." *Modern Language Quarterly.* 20 (1959)

Newman, John. *West Kent and the Weald.* Baltimore: Penguin, 1969. Plate of Father Time from Rochester Cathedral

Nicoll, Robertson W. *The Problem of Edwin Drood: A Study in the Methods of Dickens.* London: Hodder and Stoughton, 1912

Oksanna, O. Nahnybida. "From Mythology to Mythopoesis: Mythological Figures and Patterns in the Novels of Michel Butor." Dissertation, Tulane University, 1971

Ovidius, Naso Publius. *Metamorphoses.* Trans. Sir Samuel Garth. New York: Heritage Press, 1961

Plutarch, *The Lives of the Noble Grecians and Romans.* Vol.I. Trans. Thomas North. Oxford: Basil Blackwell Press, 1928

Pugin, Augustus W. *On the Present State of Ecclesiastical Architecture in England.* London: Henry G. Bohn, 1853

Pugin. *The True Principles of Pointed or Christian Architecture in England.* London: Henry G. Bohn, 1853

Roudiez, Leon. "An Ever-Widening Circle." *New York Times Book Review,* 17 December 1961

Roudiez. Michel Butor. *Columbia Essays on Modern Writers,* No. 9. New York: Columbia University Press, 1965

Saxelby, F. Outwin. *A Hardy Dictionary: The Characters and Scenes of the Novels and Poems.* London: Routledge and Sons, 1911

Scott, Geoffrey. *The Architecture of Humanism: A Study in the History of Taste.* New York: Scribner's, 1969

Scully, Vincent. *The Earth, the Temple, and the Gods: Greek Sacred Architecture.* New Haven: Yale University Press, 1962

Spencer, M.C. "Michel Butor: Literature in an Electronic Age." *Meanjin Quarterly,* 28 (Summer 1969)

Spencer. "The Unfinished Cathedral: Michel Butor's L'Emploi du Temps." *Essays in French Literature,* 6 (1969)

Tarr, Sister Muriel, C.S.A. *Catholicism in Gothic Fiction in England (1762-1820).* Washington D.C.: Catholic University of America Press, 1946

Tunnard, Christopher. *The City of Man*. New York: Charles Scribner's and Sons, 1953, Plate 42

Walters, J. Cuming. *The Complete Mystery of Edwin Drood: The History, Continuations, and Solutions*, London: Chapman and Hall, 1912

Welsh, Alexander. *The City of Dickens*. Oxford: Clarendon Press, 1971

Wright, Frank Lloyd. *The Living City*. New York: Bramhall House, 1958